RELIGION IN AND ON THE JOB

RELIGION
IN *and* ON
THE JOB

EUGENE CARR

Foreword by
THE REVEREND DR. EUGENE CARSON BLAKE
President, National Council of the Churches of Christ

COWARD McCANN, INC.
NEW YORK

Copyright, 1956, by Eugene Carr

Library of Congress Catalog Card Number: 57-7056

The Author and Publisher gratefully acknowledge the
courtesy of The Brush-Moore Newspapers, Inc. in granting permission to reprint the material in this book.

Manufactured in the United States of America

Dedicated to
Bob and A. J. and Jeanne

Contents

Foreword

ONE OF THE MOST interesting and important characteristics of the present renewal and revitalization of religion in the United States has been a sharp increase in lay activity in the life of the Churches.

In cities and towns all over the nation, there are men who only a few years ago were passive, not to say bored, members of their churches, but who today are enthusiastic leaders of other laymen in a wide variety of Christian programs, local, regional and national.

These men are reading religious books along with their Bibles. They are applying sales techniques to religious propaganda. They are learning about the programs of their denominations. More important, they are finding in Christian faith and life a satisfaction that they did not know before.

One of these new leaders in the Presbyterian Church is Eugene Carr, the author of this book. I have seen him operating not only in the national program of Presbyterian men, but also in his own home town among the men who know him best. He is a natural leader of men. Professionally he is a newspaper and radio man.

Most of the brief religious essays that follow appeared first in a newspaper column. They are authentic and professional; they communicate in the language that men understand.

This book couldn't have been written a few years ago. And even if it had been written, there would likely have been no reading public for it.

Today it will be read by many lay Christians who will find Gene Carr speaking in their own idiom to their own condition. Pastors who want to understand men in the pews will be wise to read it too.

Nothing could be better for the Christian Church than a number of such books as this written by laymen for whom Christianity is a new enthusiasm—written for laymen who need to think about their faith as well as feel it.

THE REVEREND DR. EUGENE CARSON BLAKE,
President, National Council of the Churches of Christ in the U.S.

RELIGION IN AND ON THE JOB

Two Carpenters—A Parable

Two YOUNG MEN SAT TOGETHER over their lunch one hot summer day. They were apprentice carpenters, learning their trade under the exacting supervision of an oldtime construction foreman.

They had been working in a broiling sun since early morning. They were tired, even though the day was only half gone. They didn't seem to have much interest in their sandwiches. Mostly, they sat resting, silently looking out over the city they called home.

Perhaps they thought of their work, the long hours ahead. Perhaps they thought of the busy streets where they lived, the rush of traffic, the hurry and hustle of people, the bright lights on hot nights. Perhaps they thought of the future, their hopes, their desires, their wants. Or, they may have thought of the past—the Battle of the Bulge or Guadalcanal.

They were very much like any two young Americans —former GI's, starting out on a job, married, planning for a family, earning a living.

"You know," said Jim, "I was reading in a book last night that if you decide on the three things you want most and concentrate on those three things, you'll get what you want."

"Oh yeah!" Joe responded. "Sounds mixed up to me! How can you get what you want just by thinkin' about it?"

"I don't know," Jim answered. "That's what the book said. Besides, it didn't say that you get things by just thinking. You have to concentrate."

"So what's the difference!" Joe snapped. "Thinkin' and concentratin'—they're both the same."

"Maybe not," Jim said. "Could be a difference. Maybe it depends on what you want."

Joe shrugged his shoulders and lit a cigarette.

"Tell you what let's do," Jim said, suddenly. "Let's make a list. You make your list. I'll make mine. Let's see if it works."

Finally, Joe agreed. The two took a stubby pencil and scratched out their lists on pieces of wrapping paper. Each tucked his list away in his billfold.

Several years later, Jim was getting out of his car one morning in front of a construction job he was supervising. He thought he recognized the man coming across the street. He hadn't seen Joe since that hot summer right after the war.

"Hey, there, Joe!" he called. "Where've you been keeping yourself? Working, I suppose?"

"Not too much lately," Joe answered. "But say— what's this, a new car? Yours?"

"Well—I do a lot of driving," Jim replied, "back and forth from the shop to the jobs we're handling. We're plenty busy right now. My wife was complaining the other night because I didn't have time to help her move into our new house."

Joe stood for a moment looking at his old friend. It was evident Jim was doing well—a new home, a new car, a good job.

"By the way, Jim," he said, "remember we wrote down the three things we wanted most. How'd it work out for you?"

"All right, I think," said Jim.

"Still got your slip of paper?" Joe questioned.

"Still have it—right here," Jim said, and pulled out his billfold.

"How about tradin' slips, if I can find mine?" Joe urged. "I'd like to take a look at yours."

The two men drew worn and wrinkled pieces of paper from their billfolds.

Joe's list read—

"I want a big job, a new car, a lot of money."

Jim's list read—

"I want to be a better carpenter, a good husband and father, a credit to my God."

Shall We Go to Church?

THE RESULTS OF AN INTERESTING SURVEY on the question of church attendance among employes were published some time ago in a national personnel consultants' bulletin.

The survey had been conducted in representative businesses and industries across the country. Only one question was asked— "Do you attend church regularly, occasionally, or not at all?" The work record of each individual who answered this question was then checked to determine if there might be a relationship between his church attendance and his work habits.

The survey showed approximately 50 per cent of the employes interviewed attend church regularly. One-fourth answered they attend occasionally, and the remaining fourth said, "Not at all."

When the work records were studied, it was found that in almost every instance the regular church-goer had a good record, was steady and dependable in his employment, above average in productivity, and experienced less difficulty in his life. By the same token, those who attended church only occasionally did not measure up quite so well on the job, and those who answered "Not at all" were least dependable, had the poorer production records, and were inclined toward trouble on and off the job.

Of course, this does not mean that every worker who doesn't attend church isn't a good worker. Nor does it mean that a churchgoer is necessarily a better worker than one who does not attend.

These are average figures and, without doubt, there are many fine workers who attend church only occasionally or not at all.

But it is certainly understandable that there would be a relationship between church attendance and good work habits. The challenge laid down in our churches week after week is the challenge to live right, think right and be right, and that means on the job as well as in the home and in our social contacts.

The church challenges us to be reliable and resourceful, honest in our efforts, and proud of our achievements. It challenges us to be what we know we ought to be, in our work, in our play, in all our dealings with others.

These are desirable character traits in an individual, no matter who he is or what he does. If he has them, they will be inter-related in all the facets of his life—in his church work, in his family responsibilities, and on his job. If he doesn't have them, his church is one place where he can be exposed to them.

There are many different reasons why people start going to church in the first place, but there is always and eventually one reason why they keep right on going. In the church of their choice they find an atmosphere of peace, a sense of well-being, an inspiration to look upward, and a spiritual contact with God.

An employe put it this way one day: "Sundays come just about often enough to keep me out of trouble. You see, I'm inclined to start wavering along about Friday or Saturday! Then comes Sunday and church, and I get back on the track."

Communism Can't Match It!

IT IS KNOWN THAT COMMUNIST ORGANIZERS in this country make every effort to infiltrate sensitive jobs in business and industry. They know that a strong economy and worker satisfaction do not make fertile ground in which to sow seeds of discontent. They attempt to create plant dissension, to disrupt industrial progress.

Labor Unions recognized this some years ago and have taken steps to rid their groups of subversive elements. Business and industry are constantly on the alert. Laboratories, research firms and testing centers have set up protective measures to prevent spying and sabotage.

All of this is a part of the struggle between two entirely different concepts of life. One, the communist concept, is based on dictatorship and supremacy of the State, with no allowance for the rights and dignity of man and with no room for God in his life. The other concept, our concept, is based on freedom of action for the individual, the preservation of his rights and maintenance of his dignity, blessings conferred on him by his God.

The average worker, then, has a direct responsibility today in the current struggle between these two ways of life. As a believer in God and as a recipient of His blessings, the man and woman on the job can be most effective in helping to combat the growth of the communist influence.

Actually, the communists and their highly organized apparatus can't begin to match the forces for good in our country, if these forces put their convictions to work in everyday occupational contacts.

Church groups of laymen organizations alone number in the millions. There is the Christopher movement in the Catholic Church, and the men's clubs in the National Federation of Temple Brotherhoods, and practically every large Protestant denomination now has an active laymen's group set up on a nationwide basis.

Take, as an example, just one of these groups. Earlier

this year, in a period of five weeks, this particular organization held three regional meetings of the men of its church, with the total attendance numbering some 7000. These 7000 men represented 800,000 members back home, or approximately one representative for each one hundred men in the church.

In the three meetings, 620 trained leaders, all laymen, conducted discussion programs on questions concerning the place of the church in today's problems, and drove home the importance of the application of one's religious faith to his everyday vocational pursuits.

For sheer numbers and organization, the communists can't match the power and influence of dedicated churchmen. But, unfortunately, numbers alone won't stop the inroads of communism. That's where the communists have an advantage. To date, at least, they carry more zeal and enthusiasm into their job of selling communism than the average church layman applies to his responsibility to combat it.

The church layman has one strong argument to successfully combat communism. Communism is Godless, it abolishes religion wherever it takes hold, and it permits no place for God in the lives of people under its control.

No other argument is needed. Men and women devoted to God can stop communism cold in any worker group in the United States.

Not Who But What · · ·

THE MEMBERS OF A BOARD OF DIRECTORS had been in meeting the better part of a day. The subject under discussion was what to do about an employe who had suddenly gotten himself into trouble. The question was not whether the employe was right or wrong; he was definitely in the wrong. But, he had been in the company's service many years, held an important position, and had been considered a key man. The question was —under what conditions should he be dismissed?

The discussion by board members developed into quite a heated argument. There were strong opinions voiced by those who wanted to drop the employe without any consideration, and there were equally strong opinions in favor of granting him liberal severance benefits.

These two points of view were presented so forcefully by opposing factions on the board that the differences between them, rather than the fate of the employe, became the major issue.

Finally, the president of the firm, who had quietly heard the argument and weighed it, called the meeting to order.

"Gentlemen," he said, "I am afraid we have permitted ourselves to become sidetracked. We are here to decide what is the right thing to do in this instance. The question seems to have developed into a case of which one of us is right. I'd suggest that we get back to our original purpose. We will now continue the discussion on the basis of WHAT is right among us, rather than WHO among us is right!"

Unfortunately, it is true that too often we base our judgment of people and things on the desire to be the one who makes a decision instead of a desire to be fair and just. It is a part of our nature to want to be the one who is right but it is also a part of our better nature to want to do the right thing.

We are faced every day with a possible clash between these two traits. One is bound to win out over the other, and the one that wins will be determined by the amount of self-discipline a person is capable of applying to the questions that come before him. If he has schooled and trained himself to follow rigidly the dictates of his better self, he will be honest and dependable in his actions. If not, the weaker traits of his character will prevail, and his judgment will be unreliable and damaging.

There cannot be two absolute, right sides to a question. There may be degrees of rightness, but one will be right and the other will be only partially right. If it appears there are two points of view that are equally correct, then neither will be trustworthy, for, like two positive poles, they will repel one another.

Fortunate, indeed, is the person who can detach himself from a problem and look at it dispassionately and objectively. This is not an easy thing to do because our selfish desires and personal ambitions are persistent. They insist on asserting themselves, they demand to be heard, they want to be felt. But it is possible to submerge them in favor of more desirable human qualities.

In any difficult decision we are called upon to make, we need first to stand off and look at ourselves and eliminate our own interests from the picture. Then, once we have become entirely selfless in our approach to the matter, we should listen for the Voice that comes from within all of us in times of trouble and stress, if we will but give that Voice a chance to break through the barriers of personal pride and greed.

Without doubt, the president of the board of directors in the situation recited stood to one side that day and looked at the problem independently of all company interest. Without doubt, he followed the instructions of the Voice that came from within him.

He was a fortunate man. A man is always fortunate when he is able to distinguish the difference between WHO is right and WHAT is right.

The Open Doors

NOT LONG AGO, a young man was faced with what might have been to most of us a difficult problem. The small retail store he had started when he came out of military service following World War II was in danger of losing its location.

A big, new building was to be erected in the block where he had been developing a business for nearly ten years. He would be forced to move, or give up and turn to some other line of work.

Most of his customers came from the immediate neighborhood. He had worked hard to attract them and to please them with his service. Over the years he had managed to earn a comfortable living for himself and his growing family. He did not have a big business, but he had a good business.

His problem was the risk he would take in moving, starting all over again in a strange part of town. Would he be successful? Would his old customers follow him to a location that wasn't convenient for them? Would the people in a new neighborhood accept him, want to trade with him? And where would he get the money to finance the expense of moving?

To many of us, this would have been an alarming

situation. The future would have looked dark, to say the least. There would have been a tendency to blame it on a run of bad luck, and we might even have turned sour on the world in general, and complained that we did not deserve this misfortune.

Not so the young man.

After thinking his problem through carefully, and discussing it with members of his family and a few business acquaintances, this was his answer: "All I need do is remember what my folks used to tell us kids at home—when the good Lord closes one door to you, He opens two others. A door has been closed to me. My job now is to find out why, and find one of the other doors that has been opened to me!"

God is always opening and closing doors to us. Sometimes, He does so to prevent us from making a serious mistake. Other times, He wants to test our willingness and determination to do the things He expects us to do. Perhaps He is dissatisfied with the manner in which we are using our talents and skills, so He closes a door through which we want to go and forces us to go through another. Or, He may be jarring us into a sense of responsibility in living a more purposeful and useful life.

As the young businessman concluded, God gives us a choice, the privilege of making a decision, not between good and evil, but, rather, a choice between two or more avenues of good. Our job is to seek out and find —Seek and Find—the open doors to opportunities.

No doubt, when the young man moves his store, he will have a "grand opening" at his new location, with everything bright and shiny, and will attract more customers to his business than he has ever had. He will have a great, wide front door, one that is easy to find and easy to enter.

What Dad Wants

THERE'S A MAN DOWN THE BLOCK who gets out of bed promptly every morning, pulls on his clothes, eats his breakfast, and starts off to work.

Several hours later in the day he comes home, has his evening meal, reads his newspaper, listens to a ball game, and occasionally goes to a lodge meeting or visits with friends and family.

On weekends, he is busy in the yard and garden, makes repairs and improvements around the house, and cleans up the family car. Once in a while, he takes off on a two- or three-day hunting or fishing trip, and sometime during the year he has a vacation.

On Sunday morning you find him dressed in his best

suit, shirt and necktie. His shoes are shined and his nails are clean. He is on his way to Sunday school and church, because that is where he wants to be with his wife and children on Sunday morning.

With consistent regularity, he brings home a pay-check. He doesn't see much of it, for himself that is, but that is perfectly agreeable with him. He sees it go to the storekeeper, the doctor, the banker, the insurance man, and the tax collector. He sees it come back as food on the table, clothing for the youngsters, a home in which they all live, and he knows it buys safeguards for his family, both now and in the future.

He doesn't give too much thought to all this—the day-in, day-out, week-by-week process of earning a living and providing for his loved ones. He accepts it as a normal thing, his responsibility, one that belongs to him and to him alone.

What does he want out of life?

He wants job satisfaction, a feeling that his skills are needed and useful somewhere in the world.

He wants a growing sense of independence in the fact that he is taking care of his own.

He wants more than the bare necessities of life so that his home, his wife, and his children will reflect his pride of accomplishment.

He wants his boys and girls to grow up to be good, strong, healthy men and women who will be a credit to his name, his community, his church, and his nation.

He wants to grow old without fear, suspicion, hatred,

or regret, with his hopes for the future based on nothing more material than he actually needs to be comfortable and respectable.

He wants an expanding appreciation of God, a developing comradeship with his Maker, a satisfying, gratifying mutual understanding between them.

He finds himself, as he advances in years, thinking more and more about the way his own father supported a large family—fed them, clothed them, sheltered and educated them—and he gathers new respect for the old home where he was raised and the fact that they were all provided with the essential things of life, both material and spiritual.

He thinks of his own tasks these days as fairly simple in comparison, and that causes him to offer up a prayer of thanksgiving for the blessings that have come his way.

The man we have been describing is typical of most of the Dads who are wholeheartedly and sincerely applying themselves to the job of being a good husband and father.

A Rod and a Staff

TWO MEMBERS OF CONGRESS sat in the little chapel of the Capitol in Washington. They were seated on opposite sides of the short aisle that divides the dozen or so straight-backed chairs which face an Altar Of All Faiths.

A soft light sifted through the miniature stained-glass window, and drew a golden glint from the edges of the great Bible before them. It was opened to The Twenty-Third Psalm.

On the surface, the two men had little in common. They represented different sections of the country. They were members of opposing political parties. They had conflicting views on practically every issue that came before their branch of Congress.

Both sat in deep meditation.

One had come to the chapel because he felt the need of guidance on a troublesome question. An extremely important bill was under debate. It had been introduced as a policy measure of his own party. It was a good bill but he felt it needed one strong amendment.

Should he offer his amendment and run the risk of building up opposition to the bill, impair the chances of its passage, perhaps kill it off altogether?

The other Congressman could not have known what his colleague had on his mind. He had no knowledge of the proposed amendment. Politically, he was against the bill, and certainly he would be even more opposed to the amendment!

Silently, they sat, eyes half-closed, motionless except for the rhythm of their heavy breathing. Each was unconscious of the presence of the other.

Suddenly, almost as though they had received a simultaneous signal, they left the room. Without exchanging a word, they went to the floor of the House chamber.

Later in the afternoon, after much heated debate on the bill, the one Congressman introduced his amendment. To his great surprise, the man who arose at once and gave the amendment a resounding endorsement was the Congressman of opposite party and viewpoint who had sat with him in the little prayer room.

The amendment passed by an overwhelming majority of votes from both parties. Not only did it make a good bill better but it paved the way for a much needed piece of legislation to become law.

Perhaps this incident might be looked upon as happenstance. But the members of Congress who make use of their little prayer room do not think so. They look upon their chapel as a place of retreat from the pressures and influences of material interests, and turn to its quiet stillness for a brand of wisdom, strength and courage that man, alone, is incapable of mustering.

To them, it was not by chance that the two men came away with a common will and determination to do what they thought right. Instead, they knew the two had cleared their minds of partisan consideration, had erased all thought of personal pride or selfish gain.

The things you do, the decisions you are called upon to make, are more certain when sustained by spiritual influence.

A Way of Life

ONE OF THE NATION'S LEADING NEWSPAPERS some time ago ran a front-page cartoon showing a map of the United States with a small steepled church resting on the top of it.

The caption under the cartoon in effect said our religious faith is based on confidence in the strength of our country. The artist seemed to have in mind the thought that political, economic and social forces nurture and support the spiritual force in our national life.

Actually, the opposite is true.

Our religious faith does not come from economic

prosperity or political and social stability. As a matter of historical record, nations tend to turn away from religion after an extended period of prosperity, good government, and social advancement. That's when they run into trouble.

The great danger in our country right now is that we will cease to observe a most important truth—that material well-being and unity of purpose come about through abiding confidence in a benevolent God. Faith in Him is our most valuable asset. From it, we derive all other benefits.

We have about us in the world today nations whose leaders seek to eliminate God from the lives of their people. They foster the theory that material things, both to the individual and to a nation, are the only essential ingredients to growth and development. They scorn God and His influence. They would have their people confine their faith and hope and loyalty to the heads of government, and what man alone can do for them.

The Godless approach is not new in the history of governmental experiments. It has been tried time and again in the past. It has always, eventually, failed. It will fail as long as governments come and go.

The cartoonist was on the right track when he linked our confidence in America with our confidence in God, but he should have shown the church as the foundation on which we base faith in our country, not the other way around.

President Eisenhower put this thought to us most aptly in a recent speech, when he said, "Without God there could be no American form of government, nor an American way of life. Recognition of the Supreme Being is the first, the basic expression of Americanism."

The President's statement goes back to the Declaration of Independence and the Preamble to our Constitution. It goes back to the Pilgrims who came to these shores in search of religious freedom. It is based on the teachings of the Bible which declare the rights and dignity of man, as an individual.

Someone said, one time, in explaining the success of our form of government, and the greatness of this nation and its people, "Those who came here to settle this land, came in search of God, not Gold. That has made the difference!"

It Rubs Off

IN ONE OF HIS EARLIER BOOKS, written before he became a famous novelist, Lloyd Douglas made the point that a beautiful rose placed in the midst of slovenly surroundings will brighten and beautify everything around it.

Dr. Douglas was explaining the miraculous change that took place in a rundown wayside home where the children of Israel left the ark of the covenant for a time. The inhabitants of the home got busy and fixed up the place, inside and out, so it would be more in keeping with the character of the magnificent golden ark.

How true it is that a thing of genuine and wholesome beauty, anywhere in our lives, automatically prompts us to improve everything else that is a part of us!

The contrast always favors the beautiful. Ugliness never damages or lessens the value of something really fine.

To the contrary, sordidness tends to move out when beauty moves in.

We see examples of this influence going on about us every day. A tiny baby, brought suddenly into a roomful of people, quiets and softens the behavior of the entire group. A woman of superlative qualities draws out the best that her family and friends have to offer. A man of excellent character raises the standard of ethics among his associates.

Even in little things in our routine living we find this influence at work. A housewife runs a dustcloth around a newly arrived bouquet of flowers, even though she had just finished dusting a few minutes before.

Dad refuses to drive the new car into the garage until he has cleaned out the rubbish and swept the floor. Junior wouldn't think of wearing his best slacks without polishing his shoes.

There are examples where we work, too—at the shop, the store, the office, on the farm—if we look for them.

Perhaps you know a payroll clerk who never fails to remember fellow employes with a birthday card.

Or a salesman who phones his mother every day during the lunch hour.

Or busy men who take the time to help a physically handicapped worker to the car that is waiting to take him home.

Or a woman who spends her evenings making baby clothes for young mothers with whom she works.

These are actual cases of what Dr. Douglas had in mind. A kind word, a pleasant smile, a thoughtful deed —are as a beautiful rose, prompting a warm and friendly response, lessening the tensions of a workaday world, eliminating—crowding out—sordid thoughts and unpleasant situations. But it is not the word or deed alone that counts; the example also counts for much.

Those who set such examples are making extremely valuable contributions to the places of their employment. They smooth over and make tolerable many a rough spot in the day. They plant hope where it had ceased to grow. They give meaning to courage where courage seemed fruitless.

They set a pattern for others to follow.

Soon there are more like them on the job, for, inevitably, what they do, what they are, rubs off on those with whom they come in contact.

They "dress up" everyone and everything within the scope of their benefiting influence.

"It" Won't End

"I DON'T KNOW WHERE IT'S ALL going to end. In a few years, everything we've ever known will be changed. There'll be automation, atomic power—and what will become of all the people, with the population growing the way it is!

"Frankly, it scares me. I'm kind of glad I won't be around to see it."

The man who made this statement recently is a highly successful businessman. During the past fifteen years, he pioneered and developed a new business that has become an important economic factor in our country. He is credited with accomplishing this through skill, imagination and initiative. Today, at the age of 60, he is wealthy, influential and independent.

Today, he talks like a man who has known only defeat. He is afraid of the future. In plain words—he is through, washed-up! He is a failure, in spite of past achievements.

What has come over this man? Where is the courage that led him, only a few years ago, to take a plunge that turned an entire industry upside down? Why should he talk this way, in 1955, at the dawn of a great new era of change in our life and living?

He did not think this way as a young man. He did not stop to ask where he was going, where he would be in 35 years, nor did he fear the changes he knew would come. In fact, at that time, he hoped they would come.

Either this man never really had faith in this world's scheme of things, or he lost it somewhere along the way.

In any event, he is refusing to accept an indisputable fact—and he is doing so at the very time in life when he needs most to acknowledge it—that the world will go right on changing in the future, as it has in the past.

Change is part of God's plan for us. Mankind is not perfect, and only through change can we hope to improve ourselves, both as a society and as individuals.

We have no right to want things to remain the same, for that would deny generations to come a better lot than we have known.

God means for us to discover new and exciting ways to benefit and advance life here on earth. He directs the skills and talents of those who make these discoveries. When His directions are followed, each discovery brings a change, and each change brings an improvement.

We must have a firm conviction that God is our partner in these affairs. We may have plans we call our own, and may be successful in executing them without being conscious of God's partnership, but plans of our own making will fail if they are contrary to God's wishes.

We do many things of a routine nature every day based strictly on faith. We have faith in our doctors, in those who process and prepare the food we eat, in the railroad engineer, the bus driver, and the plane pilot.

If we have faith in routine matters, why not an equal faith in the unfolding of momentous events in the future?

If youngsters have faith in things unknown and unseen, why shouldn't older men and women have a greater faith based on their years of experience, especially when that experience has been satisfying and rewarding?

Basis for Confidence

ONE OF MY FAVORITE PEOPLE is a "heater" in a steel mill. This man, now in his early seventies, still takes his regular turn five days a week at the roaring furnaces of a giant industrial plant.

We were talking not long ago about retirement. He was interested in the subject, but said he is in no particular hurry to leave his job. His boss is several years younger, so he wants to wait a couple of years and retire when his boss retires.

My friend likes to come home from the mill during nice weather and work in his yard and garden. Years ago, he raised prize asters, but more recently he has been specializing in vegetables.

He says a garden is a wonderful place to spend some time after eight hours in a steel mill; it's quiet, cool, fresh, and clean, and a good place to think things over, or, maybe, not even think at all.

He spends his evenings, especially during the winter months, with his phonograph albums. He has the most modern three-speed record player, and a large library of high-fidelity classical records. He doesn't care much for other forms of entertainment, but he makes allowance for the fact that all people do not like the same things.

This man is in excellent health, so he plans to be busy when he finishes up at the mill. He isn't sure what he will be doing then, but he thinks he might like to work in a greenhouse or help grow garden produce. However, he is going to let that decision come later. He figures he will get some help and guidance when the time comes.

He expects to do a lot more church work when he retires, even more than he does now.

He doesn't want to move away from his old home, that is, to a different climate or new surroundings. He prefers to stay among his friends, in his own neighborhood, and go to his own church. He has taken only one vacation trip in years. That convinced him he knows where he always wants to be.

My friend doesn't spend much time talking about people. He says he doesn't understand most people, that people aren't consistent, that they change from day to day in ways you don't expect, so it's a good idea not to count on them too much.

He talks a great deal about flowers and fruits and vegetables, and the sun and wind and snow and rain, and the grass and trees and shrubs, and music—and the steel mill. He says he understands all these things, including the steel mill. These things are consistent, he says, and even though they change from day to day, you know what to expect from them, and you can count on them.

And, then, he talks about God. He says he understands God. He says God is consistent, always the same day to day.

He says God has never let him down, has never disappointed or deceived him, has always been there to help him when he needed help. You know what to expect from God, he says, and you can count on Him.

It is no wonder my friend is unafraid of his job, unafraid of retirement, unafraid of growing old in years, unafraid of life today, tomorrow, and in the years ahead.

He isn't counting on things he doesn't understand. He has put his trust in things he understands, and his understanding starts with God.

Take Time

In Charlottesville, on the edge of the University of Virginia campus, is a little red brick restaurant, which, like thousands of similar eating places across the country, depends on a rapid turnover of customers to make money.

This restaurant caters mainly to the student trade, specializes in good food and service at low cost, provides a quick meal or snack between classes or before or after study hours. It accommodates very few people at any one time.

Yet, there is an unusual feature about "Buddy's" in Charlottesville.

At each counter and table space is a white paper doily with a message that reads—TAKE TIME!

Take Time To Think—it is the source of power.

Take Time To Read—it is the fountain of wisdom.

Take Time To Work—it is the price of success.

Take Time To Play—it is the secret of perpetual youth.

Take Time To Be Friendly—it is the road to happiness.

Take Time To Laugh—it is the music of the soul.

Take Time To Love And Be Loved—it is a God-given privilege.

Take Time To Give—it is too short a day to be selfish.

Take Time To Pray—it is the greatest power on earth.

Take Time To Visit—at Buddy's.

Here is a restaurant that, normally, would want its customers to finish up their meals and be on their way as quickly as possible. Only in this way, you would think, could enough people be served each day to make such a small place pay out for the owner. "Keep them moving," might very well be the policy.

Instead, Buddy invites his patrons to take their time, to rest and visit as long as they like. The waitresses are orderly and efficient, but do not hurry. The hostess does not rush a menu to you to get your dessert order. There is no pressure to pay the check and be on your way, even though others may be waiting for a table or counter space.

There in front of you is the constant reminder to take your time and enjoy the truly good things of life —work and play, laugh and be friendly, love and be loved, meditate and learn, give of yourself to others, and spend some time talking with your God.

Our waitress told us Buddy does not claim to be the originator of the message on his paper doilies. Rather, he picked up the various points, one at a time as he came across them, and put them all together for his customers, hopeful they would be led to discover some of the important secrets of happiness and success.

There is little question that Buddy is accomplishing his purpose. Every day, his message reaches hundreds of people, and if just one goes out of his place benefited and helped, he has made a solid contribution to mankind.

Without doubt, many a student from the nearby university has carried some part of this message with him into the business or professional world, and is a better citizen today because of it.

Buddy has done what any one of us can do. He has not attempted to originate a clever slogan or catch-phrase, or come up with some new and startling bit of advice. He has reached out and discovered for himself some of the basic tenets for good living, and is passing them on to others by the one means and manner available to him. And, in so doing, he is willing to run the risk that it might cost him in personal, material gain.

It is no wonder his little restaurant is a great success!

A Strong Team

THERE IS A GROWING RESPECT THESE DAYS for the person who makes a sincere attempt to apply a definite set of religious principles to everyday life.

Unfortunately, this has not always been true. Clergy-men and professional religionists, for the most part, have been held in high regard over the years, but the layman who "worked" at his religion has not fared so well at times. Too often, he was the object of derision.

Today there is wholesome faith in the individual who carries his religion into his job as well as his church. More people are committed to this practice, and, therefore, have a deeper appreciation of those who are on the same team.

It is gratifying to find so many applying God's laws for mankind in their homes, in daily occupations, and in social contacts, not merely listening to sermons on Sunday mornings. At least, they are conscious of God's presence in their lives, and this, alone, is encouraging. If it were not so, this old world would be next to intolerable.

So, the layman who looks to his trade or profession through the framework of his religion, rather than as something separate and apart from it, has entered a new era of respect and esteem. And, not only does he gain a tremendous personal satisfaction from the experience but he prompts others to have the courage to follow in his footsteps.

Of course, one's religious faith isn't always evident. Some people are reticent to witness to their beliefs. They hesitate to talk religion. This should not be the case, because most of us do not hesitate to express ourselves on politics, economic conditions, how to raise children, or any number of other important matters in our lives. Surely, religion is just as important.

Once the "ice has been broken" it is stimulating to find a firm commitment to God at work in the lives of many with whom we associate daily. We find it's a stronger team than we thought. Sometimes, we make this discovery where we least expect.

A well-known businessman surprised a roomful of friends not long ago by saying he never leaves his home in the morning to go to his office that he does not ask God to guide and direct him in his day's activities.

A young lady, only a few years out of school, was asked recently how she was getting along with her job. "Fine!" she replied. "I feel very grateful. God is good to me."

A group of office workers pause for a moment of silent prayer each day before beginning their lunch together. The hubbub of a busy company cafeteria comes to a temporary halt as these men and women take their places at a large roundtable.

It's like a rare disease. You think, perhaps, some of your friends and acquaintances have never heard of it because they do not talk about it. Then, you discover the "disease" is not so rare after all. Most of the people you know have it.

To Each His Own

Every fall several million young people return to the classroom or head for college and university campuses across the country. The annual competition for school honors begins again.

Youngsters are great competitors. They are inclined to test their skill at anything and everything that comes along. They want to excel in whatever they do. They want to win.

The alert coed starts the fall term wanting to sing in the choir, take the leading role in a play, and write for the school paper. The ambitious young man is anxious to star for the football team, basketball team, and track team, and head the student government.

This is as it should be, for only by testing himself will a student's talent and ability be uncovered and developed. But, too often, heartaches and frustrations result from these youthful ambitions, sometimes leaving deep and lasting scars.

That is where wise counsel and understanding in the home become so important. Advice, guidance and encouragement must not be left to teachers and school authorities alone. It is a primary job for parents.

We must remember that no two people are exactly

alike. No one is required to excel in all things that others do. An individual is expected to cultivate only the talents that are his. He should not want or hope to be like anyone else in every respect.

This is as true of boys and girls as grownups. The main difference is adults have learned from years of trial and error what they do best. They confine their efforts to those things they do well and eliminate from their lives what they cannot do.

Most parents have learned this the hard way, but there is an easy, simple manner in which to pass this lesson along to sons and daughters.

Bring God into any such discussion.

The talents we have are God-given, and are, therefore, worthwhile and glorious, each and every one of them, no matter how great or small.

Each is an individual possession, worthy of the best handling the possessor is capable of giving it. Each is a gift, and, like any gift, bestows praise on the Giver and calls for humility on the part of the recipient.

There is no reason for discouragement or despair because someone does something better than we can do it, or is superior where we have no aptitude at all. Certainly, there is no justification for jealousy in drawing comparisons between two people.

It is not our privilege to criticize others who have a lesser ability than we think they should have along a particular line. It is not our right to blame the person who is completely lacking in a specific skill.

Rather, we are meant to single out our own talents and concentrate on them, be grateful for them, accept the personal obligation that goes with possessing them. They are ours because they have come to us from the great Giver of all gifts. He wants nothing more from us than a full and proper use of what He has given us to work with.

Singleness of Purpose

A YOUNG MARRIED WOMAN WAS ASKED why she worked at such an ordinary job when her education and training qualified her for a much better salary and position.

"I don't want a better job," she replied. "I'm working to help my husband get through college, and I do not want a job to become more important to me than my reason for working."

This young lady had managed to grasp, at an early age, one of the truly significant fundamentals of life. She had set her mind on a single purpose. To her, it was a worthy one, and she was applying herself solely to accomplishing it. She would not be swayed from it.

She had been offered better jobs at more money. But, somehow, she knew a more attractive position, with the added comforts and pleasures it would bring, might distract her from her prime objective—her husband's education. She could have been a successful business woman. That wasn't what she wanted. She wanted a successful husband.

Today's world is full of glamorous appeals and offers that tend to entice us away from our avowed purposes and disrupt our plans for doing the things we know we ought to do. Eliminating and discarding these extraneous influences from our lives is one of the most difficult tasks we face up to, but this we must do, if we are to avoid being sidetracked constantly from our ultimate aims.

We must remember that a diamond of real value, no matter how small, need not be set in a cluster of miscellaneous filigree to be appreciated. The value is in the main stone, not the setting.

A melody of lasting beauty does not need a special instrumental arrangement in order to attract listeners. It bears repeating over and over again just as the composer conceived it.

A worthwhile purpose, like a perfect stone, requires no embellishment. A good motive, like a pure melody, becomes richer with every expression as it sets a clear and distinct theme and holds it.

We need very much to lift our purposes up and above the noise and confusion of the other melodies about us, and let the light of deep conviction and faith come in around them, and shine through the clean-cut facets of worthiness, willingness, selfless desire, and sincere determination.

Once we have shaken ourselves free from distractions and disruptions, we find, like the young married woman working to help her husband through college, that a single worthy purpose, unadorned and enduring, adds untold power to our hopes.

The Common Vocation

THE WORK WE DO FROM DAY TO DAY becomes so much a part of us and we become so much a part of it we are inclined to think of ourselves largely in terms of what we do to earn a living. In fact, a job connection is usually the principal means by which we introduce or identify one another.

"Meet Mr. So-and-So," we say. "He's an automobile mechanic." Or, "This is Mrs. So-and-So. She's a nurse at the hospital."

Almost always, when we read or hear about someone, it is his work, what he does for a livelihood, that stands out in the story.

This is all well and good, because an individual's job tells us something about him, gives us some basis for understanding him, sometimes leads to mutual interests and respect.

But to be known only for what we do in the way of work is not sufficient to fulfill our obligation and responsibility in life. Each of us should want something more to identify us and classify us in the eyes of others. We should want, first and foremost, to be known, not for what we do, but for what we are.

This is the difference between following an occupation and following a vocation.

You may be a storekeeper, a merchant. You work at your job to earn money. That's your occupation. But, if you devote your time and energy to developing your business into a highly reputable institution, worthy of the trust and confidence of your customers and fellow townsmen, then you are following a vocation.

Perhaps you are a school teacher. That's what you do to earn a living. But when you bend every effort to mold fine character and instill the desire in your students to be good citizens, then school teaching is a vocation with you, not just an occupation.

One of the significant distinctions between an occupation and a vocation is the difference between "housewife" and "homemaker." Being a housewife is an occupation. But homemaker, in the true sense of the word, is a vocation.

Occupations are not always conducive to producing the best a man has to offer. He may have limitations in what he is trying to do. His ability may be only average. He may be a misfit in his job.

But there is no limit to the development of the vocational aspects of a man's career. If his character traits are consistently fine, if his personal habits are above reproach, if his aims are high, even though his work performance is ordinary, he will make a successful vocation out of what might seem to be just another job.

We follow many different occupations, but we all have the same vocation—working at what we ought to be, not just what we want to do.

Your Balance Sheet

IN THE BOOKKEEPING PROCESS of a business or industry we use what is known as a "balance sheet" to keep us informed as to just where we stand. In this way we know how well we are doing, in what direction we are going. It is an over-all picture we are after, not merely our condition today, this week, or this month.

One page of a balance sheet lists our assets, some of which are "current," meaning they are immediately available for use. Other assets are "permanent," and we look upon these from the standpoint of long-range value.

On the opposite page of a balance sheet are the liabilities. Here we see what we owe now, what must be paid later, and what our long-term obligations amount to.

Then we come to "reserves" and "profit," and we know whether we are headed for success or failure.

Without a balance sheet at various intervals, we could very well be in trouble and not know it. Or, to the contrary, we might be doing much better than we think.

We would all do well to apply this business practice to our private lives from time to time. Too often, we are headed for trouble and do not know it. But, even more often, we are better off than we realize.

Our tendency is to estimate our condition on the basis of what is happening to us today. If we are faced with an extreme difficulty, we are inclined to think our lives have been misdirected from the beginning and will fail in the future. If we are "doing all right" at the present time, we are apt to feel we will go merrily along forever.

Thanksgiving Day is a good time to sit down with

our families and take a look at our personal balance sheets, make a list of the assets in our lives, make another list of liabilities. If we do a thorough job of searching our minds on this question, if we are entirely honest with ourselves, most of us will find that our assets far outweigh our liabilities.

A good businessman does not measure his success by his current position alone. He considers the permanent values on his books, the backlog of his inventory, his reserve strength. And he does not overlook the eventual obligations he must meet.

As individuals, we must not judge our success by current conditions only. There are permanent values in our lives, an inventory that will see us through, a reserve on which we can readily call. And we, too, have long-range obligations to meet.

You will recall, from the stories of the first Thanksgiving Day, that the Pilgrims were not only grateful to God for the fact they had managed to survive the early days of their venture, but they were amazed at the abundance of their blessings. Their harvests exceeded their fondest expectations, were so far beyond their actual necessities they were secure from want for months to come.

We know these good people looked to God every day and thanked Him for supplying their current needs. But Thanksgiving Day to them was a special day to acknowledge the abundance of their blessings and the permanence of their success. In doing so, they did not overlook their obligations to God, either their present or future obligations.

They knew how to set up and interpret their personal balance sheets.

You Can't Afford Not To

"HOW CAN YOU GIVE SO MUCH of your time to your church?"

This question is sometimes put to the man or woman active in church affairs. It is usually asked in an attitude of respect and often carries with it a note of admiration. But, almost always, the questioner is puzzled as to how anyone can find more than an hour or two in a busy week for church work. He does not question the practice.

Let's approach the question from two different angles. One approach is a realistic analysis of the amount of time available for anything we want to do. The other is more intangible but just as real to those who have experienced the result of applying themselves

totally and completely to the development of the spiritual side of their lives.

First—how much time do we have to give?

There are 168 hours in a week. Most of us, in a
week's time, spend 45 to 50 hours at our jobs, 50 to 55
hours sleeping, and 14 or 15 hours eating our meals.
That leaves approximately 50 hours for other interests
and activities.

Suppose we average four hours a day with our families, in reading and in recreational pursuits. We still
have 20 hours a week to account for.

If you are one who likes to have some time each day
to do whatever strikes your fancy or perhaps time to do
nothing at all, you can keep back an hour or so a day
for this purpose, and still have eight to ten hours left
over.

The average person, then, has what amounts to a
full working day each week to give to his church, if he
would do so. Any church would be glad to have that
much time from each of its members.

But the amount of time we give to church activities
is not nearly so important as what the giving of that
time does for us as individuals. That's where the second
approach to the question comes in.

Many a busy housewife and mother finds her home
runs more smoothly, family problems iron out more
easily, and daily chores get done more quickly, as she
dedicates a portion of her time and interest to her
church affiliation.

Business and professional men—doctors, lawyers, engineers, teachers, salesmen—people of every walk of life and occupation, experience a more ready response to their everyday efforts when they know they have first given of themselves to the church.

A day can start all wrong, only to completely reverse itself, once you have dropped everything else and taken care of that job you promised your clergyman you would do.

The most difficult day you have ever faced can turn out to be one in which problems seem to melt away, if that day begins with a task in behalf of your church.

It isn't important to know or understand how this happens. It's important only to know and understand that it does happen.

It isn't a question of how you can give so much time to God's work. It's a question of whether you can afford NOT TO!

Go on Record

THERE IS SOME DIFFERENCE OF OPINION as to whether a person should openly express himself on the subject of his religious faith. We sometimes hear it said that religion is strictly a personal matter, and should not be discussed in the normal course of business and social activities.

True, we should not attempt to force our ideas on others, particularly those who might be resentful. Nothing is to be gained through such a practice. And, certainly, it is not necessary constantly to let others know we try to follow a definite set of principles leading to a good way of life. The life we live should speak for itself.

But there are two important values to be gained in putting ourselves on record with those with whom we associate every day.

The first value comes to those with whom we put ourselves on record. By speaking out at the appropriate time, a fellow worker, a friend, or an associate may well receive just the encouragement he needs to direct him to a new set of standards in his life.

An example of this is a Washington lawyer who dictates a letter from time to time to a member of his family or a business acquaintance, declaring his faith in God and what his religion has meant to him. Through these letters, his secretary became interested. If religion meant so much to him, if it played such an important role in the life of this highly successful man, perhaps it could mean something to her. She became active in a church, and found what she was looking for.

The other value has to do with what it does for us.

When we put ourselves on record in anything we do, we try harder to make good. If we tell the boss we are going to make a big sale before the week is over, we concentrate on making that sale. If we say we are going to top the league in bowling this season, we work harder than ever before to be a good bowler. If we make a promise to our children, we do everything possible to make good on that promise.

It works exactly the same way in going on record as an advocate of the principles of good living as set forth in the religious faith of our choice. Once on record with a fellow worker, friend, or family, we try harder to live up to our declared intentions.

Of course, it should not be necessary to be on record with anyone other than God. Once we promise Him we will do our best day by day to live up to His hopes for us, that should be the only promise needed. But we know God is forgiving; He will give us another chance. So, we forget our promise, take advantage of His forgiveness.

On the other hand, man is not so forgiving, is not so ready to grant another opportunity. And, unfortunately, sometimes we try harder to please man than God.

Put yourself on record with your family, friends, and associates on the job. You'll find the right time and place to do so. Let them know where you stand on the subject of religion in your life.

60

Having done so, you will experience a satisfying disciplinary control over your every act and deed, a control you will not want to be without.

The High Resolve

A GOOD FRIEND RECENTLY SPOKE of how he had managed not to smoke for more than a year.

"I give it up one day at a time," he said. "Every morning I swear off for just that day. I don't make any promises for tomorrow or the next day. I don't think about how long it has been since I smoked. I take each day as it comes."

As we face the New Year, we could ask for no better pattern to follow in re-establishing our aims and setting the standard for the life we hope to live in the weeks and months ahead. We live one day at a time. We need only live up to our promises one day at a time.

The football coach who takes his team into a championship bowl game will tell you he is there because he played his schedule to win each single game throughout the regular season. A golfer knows that his drive off the first tee is just as important as his final putt.

Life is like that. If we do a good conscientious job day by day we find ourselves piling up a record of consecutive days that soon amount to a successful year. If we try to improve our lives one day at a time an over-all state of living that is satisfying and beneficial gradually unfolds and takes on permanence.

It is important, of course, to plan ahead for accomplishing the things we want to do, but the best-laid plans won't get us where we want to go if we do not give careful thought and attention to each single detail along the way. We never reach our goals unless we take the necessary steps leading to those goals.

Most of us are convinced of the desirability of applying the principles of our religious faith to the daily incidents and duties in our lives. It is something we sincerely want to do. We know there is satisfaction and reward in the practice. But do we do it, day by day, wholeheartedly, and without compromise?

Do we look forward to the time when the life we live will be recognized as top-rate, but neglect the contests we encounter during "the regular season"? Do we relish the thought of the ultimate goal we want to reach, but fail to train and practice for the daily test?

Where do we start? When do we begin? The answer is "Here and now."

This is the one high resolve we can make on New Year's Day that is worthy of our best effort—to carry our religious beliefs into and through the work days of the week, one day at a time. No other resolution lends itself so readily to a day-to-day application.

With it, each day becomes another rewarding page in the current chapter of the book that is life as we truly want to live it.

Measuring a Man

MOST OF US ARE QUICK to form opinions of other people, who and what they are, what they do and say. Usually, our approval or disapproval is decidedly strong from the beginning, based on an immediate reaction or first impression. For the most part, we rely on what is known as "snap judgment."

Yet isn't it true that often we do not have any real basis for our opinions of others? Perhaps we know only one side of the story. Our information may be completely lacking as to background, motives, personal problems, and character traits. We tend to permit emotion rather than reason to mold our thinking.

Consequently, we fall into the dangerous practice of underestimating the true worth of many people with whom we come in contact. For the emotions are not reliable when it comes to judging others. Ask the prize fighter who enthusiastically challenged the champion before he was ready to do so!

Frequently, we hear someone say, "I don't know why I should do anything to help so-and-so out of his trouble! He wouldn't help me!"

How sure are we, in a situation of this sort, that the other fellow would not come to our assistance? Have we judged him correctly, put a proper estimate on his willingness to be a friend in need? Or do we merely let our emotions overrule our reason?

When a fellow employe is late to work, or goes home early, or does not show up on the job at all, what do we think about him? Do we quickly label him as indifferent or lazy, one who readily takes advantage of his boss and the other workers in his department? Or do we give him the benefit of the doubt until we really know?

In most cases, it is not our right to pass judgment on others, and when we do find ourselves with such a right, it becomes a profound responsibility, not a privilege.

A truly great business executive followed a most interesting practice in this respect during his career. When faced with an important decision involving one of his employes or associates, he would write down all his thoughts and opinions about the individual in question. He listed good points and bad points, analyzed personal peculiarities and characteristics, and ended his review of the question by stating what he thought his decision might be. Then he would lay his analysis aside and try to forget it.

A few days later, he would come back to it, read and re-read it, sometimes read it aloud to himself. It had to make sense! It had to ring true! He knew it had to be convincing to him before it would be convincing to any one else!

This man believed in and put to use three basic principles when called upon to measure another man's worth. He sought out the highest level of conduct and character on which to base his opinion, not the lowest. He judged according to spiritual values, which know no limitation, as well as material accomplishments, which are limited by degrees of skill and ability. He knew he must have strong convictions about himself before he could have strong convictions about another.

Long-Awaited Challenge

CONSIDERABLE CONCERN IS BEING EXPRESSED these days by professional churchmen as to whether the great upsurge of interest in religion now sweeping the country really means anything.

Numerous magazine and newspaper articles have dealt with this question in recent months. Religious leaders, scholars and theologians are discussing it from the pulpit and convention platform, and on radio and television. It seems to narrow down to— "Have people actually committed themselves to God, or are they merely seeking relief from their worldly troubles?"

Fears are expressed that the emphasis on religion today may be nothing more than a "popular movement," a follow-the-crowd psychology at work, and that the whole thing may fizzle out in time due to a lack of genuine dedication on the part of the individual churchgoer.

One commentator describes America's religious look as "sleek, bouncy, and well-fed," as though these were undesirable signs of spiritual health. Another views with alarm what he calls the tendency to accept faith in God simply as a necessary ingredient in a well-adjusted, integrated personality.

Meanwhile, millions of church members and lay church workers do not seem to be nearly so concerned over the question. They continue, week after week, to devote themselves—their time, their energy, and their money—to organized church programs and responsibilities that serve as a medium of expression for their faith.

The church layman is greater in number, percentagewise to population, than any time in history. More than half of them attend church regularly. They are spending an unprecedented amount on new and remodeled church buildings, and contributing more to church budgets and benevolence than ever before.

They are reading more religious books and periodicals, attending more religious movies, and tuning in more religious radio and TV broadcasts. Even the calendar makers tell us that calendars with religious pictures and themes lead all other requests.

Isn't this proof that people are gaining something from the religious atmosphere in which they spend so much of their time these days? Aren't they showing themselves to be susceptible to an influence that can lead to a deep and lasting dedication? Suppose they have turned to God, in the beginning, as an escape from the sordid and ugly things of life! Isn't that better than if they had not turned to God at all?

The director of a large layman's organization recently reported on a ten-day trip covering three states during which he met and talked with more than 2000 men. He said, in effect— "Anyone discouraged or lacking in zeal should have come along on this trip. Clear-eyed men, committed to the task of telling the Good News, give evidence of a new day and a new hope. One of the refreshing values was the way men are using their heads and their skills to be enthusiastic witnesses to their faith."

Isn't it conceivable there would come a time when

mankind would accept God's Plan for him on this earth? This could be the time. This could be the place. It's a long-awaited challenge.

No Better Evidence

THROUGHOUT THE COUNTRY TODAY, hundreds of business firms, large and small, are stressing the need of religion in meeting and solving the problems that confront them, their employes, and the public in general. They are doing so openly—in advertising, in contacts with associates, and through services they render the communities in which they do business.

Week after week, several dozen companies in a number of different cities band together to sponsor advertisements urging church attendance and setting forth the principles that lead to a well-adjusted life of peace and contentment. These advertisements appear regularly in newspapers and are heard over radio coast to coast.

Individual firms support projects with the express purpose of promoting brotherhood, tolerance, honesty

in dealings, and fair play. Special messages from executives and management state specifically the company's
adherence to these ideals.

Several industrial organizations have now added spiritual counselors to their staffs, to help the employe
"get well" from personal problems that trouble him, in
exactly the same way the plant doctor takes care of his
physical ills and injuries.

This growing trend is most encouraging, for it means
that business institutions are willing to put themselves
on record in favor of practices that are geared to a high
moral standard. They can't very well recommend such
an approach to others and not adopt it in their own
dealings.

That is one of the important functions of advertising
as we know it today. Not only does it tell us where we
can find what we want to buy, but it also gives us some
basis for estimating the true worth of the firms we pa-
tronize. When an advertiser tells us his product or
service is of high quality, he must make good on his
claim or customers lose faith in him. The businessman
knows this, whether he is advertising peaches and pears
or stating his religious convictions.

A recent survey indicates that more and more business leaders recognize the need for maintaining employe and public confidence in what they believe as
well as what they can accomplish on the economic
front. And, in establishing the base on which they hope
to inspire this confidence, they have found there is no

better evidence than their own faith in God and the application of the teachings of the Bible.

From a simple interpretation of the Golden Rule to a deep and penetrating belief in the need for God's ever-present help, a whole new world of understanding is open to businessman, employe, and customer, alike.

The Purpose of Struggle

IT IS EASY TO BELIEVE that some people bring trouble upon themselves—reap the harvests they sow—but, often, those who are innocent of any wrongdoing are called upon to endure misfortune and injustice. Why? Certainly, man is not meant to live a life of unhappiness and despair!

Why, then, is mankind subjected to trials and tribulations? What is the purpose of struggle, so common to everyday life? There must be a reason for it.

There is an old saying that nothing worthwhile comes easily. This can be applied to gaining a material objective, or meeting a situation that calls for spiritual fortitude. In either case, the result is more permanent, more substantial, and more satisfying, if, first, obstacles and adversity have been overcome.

Wrestling with a problem, whether routine in the day's work or imbedded in personal disaster, is a test of strength, patience, and faith, a test measured in willingness to try, confidence of success, and ability "to take it." It is a stimulant to courage, a spur to incentive, a challenge to understanding. Or it should be.

Occasionally, a person who has just been struck by a serious difficulty or affliction will exclaim, "What did I do to deserve this!"

The fallacy in this thinking is in looking upon misfortune as punishment rather than an opportunity to rebuild, readjust and re-evaluate life. Out of such circumstances can come the realization of a great new faith and hope. With a proper approach, a determined struggle against odds will produce remarkable rewards.

Not long ago, a fine, godly man suffered a great loss in his family. As days passed, his friends noted there was no change in him, no deviation from his normal, accustomed habits, no visible sign of grief, no variance in the firmness of his faith. Later on, when questioned about his reactions, he said, "I am waiting for that certain day, far in the future, perhaps, but sure to come, when I will understand."

No one in recent years suffered more disappointment, criticism, and trouble than Abe Lincoln. Yet he struggled on with the problems and difficulties of his time.

He knew each of the hardships he bore had a purpose back of it.

The American Negro, who gained his freedom during the historic conflict of Lincoln's day, has struggled for the fruits of that freedom. Out of this struggle has emerged a people who have made more progress than any race in history in so short a time.

There is no necessity for standing heavy in our shoes, weighed down by burdens, when a great Power is waiting to give us a spiritual lift along the way. The important thing is to enlist that Power on our side in the struggles of life.

Davey Could Pray

DAVEY WAS A BIG MAN, with a thick neck set on a rough-hewn frame that pivoted on a pair of swaggering hips. His hands were tough and muscles strong from many years of hard work.

Davey was a railroad switchman. He was a good railroad switchman. He was also good in a fight. He knew how to use his fists.

Davey hadn't always been a praying man. But a family tragedy half-way through life jerked him up short. He wasn't home at the time. He was needed and couldn't be found.

He turned to a church for the answer to his grief. He found what he was looking for. He became a presiding elder, and, in line with his office, was called upon from time to time to pray.

There he would stand before the congregation, eyes closed, unconscious of the presence of any one other than his God.

Davey never prayed for things. Rather, he asked God for strength and patience and wisdom and self-control. He never asked God to solve his problems for him. He asked only for help in solving his problems for himself. And he never asked for help unless his purpose was worthy.

He did not expect the world to be shaped to suit him. He knew this wouldn't work. He knew he must shape his life to fit the world as God wanted it. He would say so in his prayers.

Davey did not ask for blessings of a material nature. He didn't expect prayer to take the place of work. He knew he had to be on his job in the switching tower if there would be food on the table and clothing for the family. He came to look upon his job as a blessing.

In all the praying he did in public, he was never known to pray for himself. He prayed for others—his neighbors and fellow townsmen, the church and the clergy, those whose lives had fallen upon sorrow and misfortune, those who had not come to know God. But he also included happy situations and the pleasures of living in his prayers. He turned to God in joy as well as sorrow.

Davey prayed as though he knew his prayers would be answered, and they were answered, because he confined his prayers to things he knew God was interested in.

There were those in the congregation who criticized Davey. Some called him a hypocrite because he had not always been a praying man. When this did not stop Davey, they said he prayed too long. But Davey kept right on, and included his critics in his prayers.

A childhood memory sometimes serves as the strongest tie we could possibly have in the daily challenge to live the good life as it should be lived. Such a tie is the memory of Davey's prayers.

It's Good for the Heart

DUE, NO DOUBT, to President Eisenhower's attack some time ago, we have been literally deluged in recent months with advice and information on heart trouble. Almost every day we have occasion to read about a new study on the subject, or listen to an up-to-date opinion from an authority.

This is all to the good, for there is no question that heart trouble has become a major threat to man's well-being, and the more we know about it, the more we hear it discussed and analyzed, the better prepared we will be to cope with it when it comes, or avoid it altogether.

There was a time when heart disease was identified for the most part with older people, the person whose natural life was about spent. Doctors used to say that such a person died because his heart gave out—"heart failure," it was called.

But heart trouble today is no respecter of age or sex or occupation. It strikes young and old alike, women as well as men, and is common to factory worker, store clerk, housewife, and business executive.

Today, a perfectly healthy heart is subject to attack with little or no warning. The experts say this is due to our current mode of living, the speed we travel, the pace of the business day, the fact we play as hard as we work, the intensity with which we approach almost everything we do. Psychologists tell us there is also a factor of insecurity in all this, that the average person seems to sense an impending disaster or danger to himself and those for whom he is responsible.

Perhaps this is true. Without question, life is more

complicated than in days gone by. But there are also more conveniences and comforts in present-day living, and no one does the hard, physical labor that once took its daily toll of his strength. What, then, is the answer? Where do we look for relief from the worry, pressure, and tension that bring on so many of today's heart attacks?

The specialist invariably recommends three things— sufficient rest, proper diet, and mild exercise. But physical rest is of little use without peace of mind, diet is of no value unless accompanied by a sense of well being, and exercise is worthless if pressure and tension remain.

A heart attack, or any other serious illness, should serve as a warning that the time has come to re-evaluate life, place the proper emphasis on our desires and wants, our purposes and ambitions. With it should come a new sense of humility, a realization that mere man is not a super being, is not essential to all things or capable of everything.

We must listen to the medical doctor. But we must also turn to the Master Physician. We must give Him a chance to play His part in the diagnosis and cure. If we do so, then will come the security and confidence and faith that permit a physical restoration to take place effectively and completely.

Young People Want It!

MUCH OF THE EMPHASIS on juvenile delinquency today can be traced to a tendency to read and remember the bad things youngsters do, and read and forget the good.

True, on the average day, your newspaper will have a story about a teenager who is in trouble. But, likewise, day after day, we have the opportunity to read of a worthwhile project or a genuinely good deed in which a youngster or group of young people is involved.

Here are some examples taken from the news recently:

A seventeen year old girl and three boys were arrested for a series of holdups. The same paper carried a story and picture of four high school students planning a Brotherhood Week program for their school.

A fourteen-year-old boy confessed the murder of a neighborhood playmate. Across the page was a story of a twelve-year-old who received an award for saving the life of a small child.

Law enforcement officers announced they had rounded up a youthful gang accused of a series of juvenile crimes. The same evening, four boys in the same area became Eagle Scouts.

One day, two pictures appeared on a front page. One picture showed college students demonstrating over a racial problem. Next to it was a picture of a Negro student and a white student taking the same test in a general information quiz.

The point here is that young people are doing worthy, useful things which are reported to us every day, but the adult reader fails to place the same importance on the good as the bad.

There is an old saying that 90 per cent of the trouble in the world is caused by 10 per cent of the people. Without doubt, this is as true in the teen-age group as among grownups. Far more youngsters spend their time and energy in honorable and lawful pursuits than in unlawful and troublemaking activities.

Ask your clergyman how many young people of high school and college age are active in the youth groups of his church. You may be surprised at the answer. In one case, nearly 70,000 teenagers participated in the youth organizations of one denomination in one state alone last year. You can duplicate that figure in several denominations in state after state across the country.

Reports indicate the greatest demand in history for religious courses and training in our colleges and universities. In one survey, 80 per cent of the students asked said they felt the need for a firm religious faith.

These are the fathers and mothers and citizens of the future. They deserve our recognition for the fine job they are doing in building their lives on a solid foundation. They deserve to have the stories about them—who they are and what they do—not only read, but remembered.

A Daily Question

"How can i adhere 100 per cent to a set of religious principles and still get along in the world in which we live today?"

Have you asked yourself this question? Does it bother you?

Do you wonder how you can reconcile the basic tenets of a religious faith to some of the social customs and business practices we encounter from day to day?

Each of us is called upon to face up to this question almost every day. It challenges business and professional people. It becomes involved in the relationships of friends and neighbors, student and teacher, members of families, and, certainly, it has a bearing on job competition between fellow workers.

It points its finger to selfishness and greed as evidenced in routine procedures of the workaday world.

It reveals itself in the plotting for personal gain. It is a question to be asked in the corporation conference room, the employe committee meeting, the shop, the store, the office, the home.

Some of us put this question to ourselves as a declaratory statement—"How can I?"—admitting there is nothing to do but go along with prevailing custom, that to do otherwise would bring economic suicide and personal disaster.

Others sincerely want the answer to—"Can I be honest, always, under any and all circumstances? Do I dare be forthright and aboveboard in my dealings? If so, will I lose out?"

It is not a sign of weakness to be concerned with this question. In fact, the person who is conscious of it has recognized the conflict between his spiritual and material existence, and has taken the first important step in meeting the temptations of worldly environment.

Life is not easy. It has never been easy. There is a continuing struggle between good and bad influences. The human tendency is to take the short cuts, compromise principle to practice, only to find this to be the roughest road of all.

The tests that come every day are many and varied. They range from an idle word of unfair criticism to a major attempt to deceive and destroy. They are found in a hollow gesture of good will, the acceptance of a dishonest favor, the pursuit of an unwarranted ambition, the unethical move for an undeserved advantage.

Usually, they are clothed in the ill-founded excuse—
"Well, in this case, the means justifies the end!"

The means never justifies the end unless the end is
supported by a worthy purpose. We can gain an advantage from time to time by placing expediency ahead
of principle, but the advantage gained can be nothing
more than temporary, and the ultimate result will be
added hardship and difficulty.

In the final analysis, the daily question that confronts
us should not be whether we can, but whether we can
afford not to try to get along in this world, and still live
up to the professed principles of our religious faith.

A Proper Perspective

ONE OF THE PRONOUNCED CHARACTERISTICS of a truly
great man is the ability to stand aside, away from the
entanglements of daily routine and influence, and
measure his work in terms of ultimate objectives and
purposes. By so doing, he avoids the pitfall of placing
his own importance over and above the importance of
what it is he is supposed to accomplish.

This, more than anything else, accounts for the fact that a man who has risen to high station in life becomes less concerned with personal credit and tribute as he becomes more concerned with the overall success of the venture in which he is engaged. To him, the final result is the important thing, not the fact he has been important to it.

Look at it this way—as a plane climbs higher and higher in the sky, it casts a smaller and smaller shadow on the earth below. Yet the high-flying plane speeding aloft on powerful engines is far more vital to the success of air travel at the moment than the plane sitting over its own shadow on the ground.

It is all a matter of perspective. We must learn to stand aside and look at ourselves in relation to the whole of life, our value to others and what we might do for them, not strictly their value to us. We must resist the temptation of thinking something is important because we have made it so. More likely than not, it was important in the first place, before we had anything to do with it, and we became important because of an association with it.

We could want no better example than the story which lies behind our observance of Palm Sunday.

The stage was all set for a new King to take over. The people gathered together in anticipation of a triumphant and victorious overthrow of the established regime. They were ready for a change, by popular demand and acclamation.

But it did not happen that way. There was no pomp or show of strength. There were no rousing speeches or exhortation to revolt, no appeal to mass psychology.

This was not the purpose of the new King. He knew His ultimate objective. He did not lose sight of what was expected of Him. His own importance was lost in the importance of His true place in the life of man.

He was concerned with the size of the task to be performed, not the size of the shadow He might cast around Himself.

Let the Bells Ring

THERE IS A THRILLING MOMENT that comes every Sunday morning to those who attend church. It is the moment before church begins, before the choir has sung a note, before the clergyman has said a word.

It comes with the closing strains of the organ prelude. The light seems a little softer. The walls seem to move in a little closer. The people are more together. Murmurs cease, and a quiet peace settles over the assembly.

Then, the first great bell starts to ring. And it is

joined immediately by a second and a third and a fourth, until a mighty chorus of bells and chimes fills the air with a glorious intonation. Another Sunday morning has come. God is in His heaven and His people have gathered to worship Him.

The organ joins the volume and grows in force as the bell tones fade away, to be replaced by the majestic notes of the opening hymn. Church has begun. The bells have told us so as only church bells can tell us.

It is a thrilling moment. Those who attend church have an opportunity to experience it, sense it, feel it.

On Easter Day church bells will ring with special significance. The tones will be clearer and stronger, and the thrill that comes with their ringing will have a sharper meaning. Every living thing will stir, as a new burst of life springs from the earth to join a new faith and a new hope in the hearts of men. Everything, without and within, will come alive, fresh and clean.

This will be Easter Sunday, a day of joy and happiness, a day of triumph and victory.

Then will come Monday.

Monday will be another day. We will go to our jobs, to the shop, the store, the office, the farm, the classroom. We will busy ourselves with duties in the home. Church bells will not ring as on Sunday morning, as they rang the day before to welcome another Easter.

But we can hear the bells on Monday if we will. We can hear them on Monday, and on every other day of the week. We can hear them in the request of a friend, the plea of a child, the voice of a loved one. They can echo in a smile, a kind word, a thoughtful deed. We can intone their meaning in our attitude and conduct toward others.

The bells of Easter can ring for us throughout the week, day after day throughout the year. We need not ever be without the message in their ringing.

Freedom From Fear

FOR TWENTY YEARS OR MORE, we have been steadily following in the United States a program intended to bring security to the lives of our people. This program has been based, primarily, on a philosophy that we should be free from fear and anxiety at all times, regardless of circumstance or condition.

Of course, certain elements of fear are not included in this program. The intuitive type fear that comes with facing sudden disaster or danger, for instance, or the brand of fear that prevents us from walking into the pathway of a speeding automobile. Such fears serve a useful purpose and often save us from bodily injury or physical harm. They are not involved in the philosophy of freedom from fear.

The brand of fear we have been attempting to eliminate from our lives is something else. It is the fear of want or need—apprehension over economic problems, concern with health matters, dread of tomorrow and what it might bring. We have been striving for a permanent sense of well-being. But, apparently, we have missed the mark, for, after all these years, there never has been a time when so many people were afraid of what might happen to them!

Could it be, in our efforts to escape from fear, we have run away from the greatest source of freedom from it?

Our experiment certainly proves that no amount of economic planning, no set of security measures, will bring peace of mind or mental assurance. More safeguards against loss of job and income, against sickness and disability, are in effect today than any time in history. Yet people worry that want and illness will overtake them, and dread the advancing years.

What's the answer?

During the recent Lenten season, we had occasion to read a story about a man who started selling newspapers as a small boy to support a widowed mother and four younger brothers. Over the years, he saved some money, invested and reinvested it, until he was worth two million dollars. But, in spite of his wealth, some-

86

thing told him to stay on his corner selling papers.

When the stock market crashed in 1929, he lost his two million dollars in eight days. Then he had his answer. He knew he had been afraid to change for fear he would forget God as the source of all good things. He took his financial loss in stride and went on to live a happy, useful life, founded on a deep-rooted religious faith.

The only sure way to take fear out of living is to keep a respectful fear of God in our lives, which means to maintain a reverent attitude toward His place and influence in the scheme of things. This brand of fear is a healthy ingredient, a deterrent to want, a spur to courage and confidence, an insurance against loss, a source of comfort and understanding at any age. All other fears are snuffed out when a proper fear of God dominates us.

Champion House Cleaner

IT'S SPRING CLEANING TIME AGAIN, and at least one housewife is happy about it.

This remarkable lady is actually looking forward to the annual chore so many dread—scrubbing and polishing, painting and papering, the disorder and confusion of dustpans and mops, buckets and barrels, bare floors and misplaced furniture. Not only will she turn her own little house upside down and clean every nook and corner of it, she will help other housewives do the same in their homes. For this woman adds to her family income throughout the year by working a day or two each week cleaning house for others.

There never has been anyone quite like her. She goes into a home and systematically washes, scrubs, polishes, and cleans each room. She removes spots from furniture, mends chipped china, repairs a kitchen utensil, sorts out and disposes of old papers and magazines. You will find her on top of a stove cleaning an exhaust fan, sitting in a window washing storm sash, sills, and screens, or high on a stepladder adjusting a chandelier. If a slipcover needs laundering, it suddenly disappears, to return in a few days fresh and new.

The point to all this is, here is a woman who gives everything she has to offer to the type of work left for her to do. She puts it this way— "I can't do anything but clean house, but, if I do say so myself, I know how to clean a house!"

As a matter of fact, she has many talents. She sews well, makes beautiful artificial flowers, is an expert gardener, and has a fine sense of color combinations. She is especially adept at making attractive gifts and useful gadgets from the odds and ends most people discard. But, rather than being unhappy because she is not a recognized artist or successful designer, she applies all her skill to the job she is doing.

This champion of all house cleaners is a woman of great pride; not pretense, but pride—there's a difference! When she walks out of a house at the end of a long, wearisome day, there's a smile on her lips and a look of triumph in her eyes. There is happiness in her voice as she says "goodby." She is proud of what she has done. She feels good that on this day she has brought comfort and pleasure to others. It is no wonder she says, "I like to clean house!"

It will be only a few short weeks now until she will start out from her home early in the morning for a day of work, with a bouquet of freshly cut flowers from her garden to add to the beauty of the home she will clean, and bring more happiness to those she serves so well.

Accentuate the Positive

RECENTLY, a casual conversation between two friends covered the following bits of "news":

(1) The difficulty a father and mother were having with their young daughter—

(2) The criticism being leveled at an employer by one of his employes—

(3) The dissatisfaction of a church membership with one of the organizations of the church—

(4) The quarrel between two business partners—

(5) The reason why a certain family moved out of town.

The entire conversation probed and pried into the personal affairs of their friends and acquaintances. It was marked by accusations and fault-finding. Apparently, in this case, there wasn't anything good to say about anyone!

What a wonderful thing it would be if we would all come out of the shadows and get on the right side of the sun in our attitude and thinking toward others. If we would only try it, for just one day, one entire day with emphasis on the good to be found in the world, the possibilities for happiness among men would be tremendous. Here's what would happen—

We would go off to work in the morning, anxious to get there, full of enthusiasm for the day ahead. We would pitch in and get our jobs done, and turn in the best possible work performance. We would give credit to our fellow employes, the foreman or supervisor in charge, management and ownership, and the economic system that makes our jobs vital and important.

We would go home at the end of the day, grateful for the privilege of work, grateful for the homes and families awaiting us. We would have time for the children and their interests. We would be sympathetically concerned over the welfare of neighbors and friends. We would be glad to hear good news about them.

We would enter into the affairs of our church to lend a hand in the tasks to be performed. We wouldn't expect someone else to be a better member than we try to be. We would be proud of our church affiliation and our identification with its place in the community.

We would say good things about our town and help build it in a manner to inspire others to say good things about it.

We would search ourselves, honestly and sincerely, in an effort to cultivate and strengthen the better side of our lives and eliminate the sordid and unpleasant.

We would accept our own limitations of talent or skill, personal attributes, and material means for exactly what they are—limitations that restrict certain channels of progress so other channels will flow fully and freely on to fulfillment.

In all things, we would seek first the reasons why, not the reasons why not; we would look first for the good, not the bad; we would accentuate the positive, not the negative.

Pathway to Patience

PATIENCE IS A VIRTUE. Or so we are told and have been told in literature, song, art, and sermon almost since the beginning of time.

Fortunately, patience is not the only virtue, or else man today would be next to devoid of virtue. We are probably the most impatient slice of humanity ever to inhabit the earth.

Perhaps this is due to the jet-propulsion age in which we live. Everything is moving faster and faster, including the human machine. Or it may be we are simply trying to do more, crowd an increasing number of activities and interests into the hours of the day, which have not lengthened either in time or number.

In any event, we aren't as patient as we should be

and need to be with the unfolding of life, whether it be a life span or a single day in a life span.

We see this trait in the automobile driver who sneaks around a red traffic light, only to have the light turn green four seconds later. We see it in annoyance with a disconnected phone call, a late appointment, or an untimely interruption, without a good reason most of the time for becoming annoyed. We see it in the youngster who is impatient to grow up, and we see it in older people who are impatient with the impatience of youth.

Most of us are impatient because we are mixed up in our overall planning. When young, we plan too far ahead. When we reach the advanced years, we do not plan far enough. So, at every stage of life we run the risk of frustration because something does not happen as we planned it to happen, or because nothing happens because we did not plan something to happen.

Planning is essential to a well-ordered life, but there are two important things to remember about plans.

First of all, plans seldom materialize exactly as planned. They are constantly being changed by forces beyond our control. The test is in our capacity to adjust to change, to regulate our hopes and ambitions to new circumstances, and exercise self-control over disappointment.

Secondly, we do not always know what is best for us, even though we might think we know. Very often, the most promising development of the moment proves later to be something we would not want at all, as a new and exciting interest of which we had never dreamed moves in on us. The test is in our faith.

If you believe God plays a part in your life and actually has a specific set of plans for you as an individual, then you have the only justification you need for practicing patience. For your plans are not better than His. Your plans will not work if they are not co-ordinated with His. What you might want is so much froth, unless it is also what He wants.

One of the Biblical Psalms tells us a good man is like a tree by a river that brings forth its fruit in due season. There stands the tree, unbloomed and barren, watching the river roll by day after day, until, finally, the right season comes along. Then, and then only, the tree brings forth its fruit. In the meantime, it has remained calm and composed, undisturbed by the impatient waters rushing down to the sea.

Each of us, too, is meant to have a fruit-bearing season in the scheme of things, if we successfully resist the rushing tide of man-made impatience.

An Exact Science

A GROUP OF AMERICAN CLERGYMEN returned from the Soviet Union recently and announced that one of the reasons the government there has stepped up its curriculum in scientific and engineering education is the hope of ultimately wiping out all interest in religion on the part of the Russian people.

Apparently, the Red leaders believe science and religion are completely incompatible, and that once they have swung their nation over to a predominantly industrial economy, religion will become submerged in a mass of factual data and mathematical standards.

They are doomed to disappointment. They need only to look to the United States, where scientific development and industrial growth have set the pace for the rest of the world, to learn how very wrong they are in their thinking.

As our nation has changed from an agrarian to an industrial economy over the past 40 to 50 years, we find interest in religion here has not merely moved up at a rapid rate, but actually has been in the forefront of scientific discovery and engineering skill. Today's picture needs no elaboration. With church membership and activity at an all-time high, industrial productivity and scientific development have never been greater.

Likewise, today, there is a growing volume of evidence that men of science find their occupational interests to be entirely compatible with a religious faith. More and more of them are crediting the power and influence of a Supreme Being with the success of their efforts.

A prominent engineer in a large industrial firm is now writing his second article on this subject for a magazine published in his particular field. A young scientist, just out of school and working as a laboratory chemist, expressed it this way not long ago: "I believe in the electron, even though I've never seen one. I've never seen God, but I can still believe in Him!"

A world-famous astronomer closes his lecture to his senior class each year by pointing up the importance of religious faith as a guide to the good life, and spiritual insight as a source of strength. One of the greatest inventors of modern times thought of the actions of the earth's elements as demonstrations of God's power.

The men in the Kremlin are in for a surprise. They will find, as their crop of young scientists and engineers grows and matures, there will come a time when the doors of discovery unlock for them in a way beyond the understanding of mere man. Then will come the belief that religion, too, is an exact science to those who have faith.

Most Honored Profession

A VERY WISE WOMAN used to say that three professions have always stood out above all others in service to mankind.

The first, she would explain, is the medical profession, for "doctors save men's lives." Her second choice was the school teacher who "develops men's minds." Then she would single out the clergyman and his specific responsibility for "saving men's souls."

Since this woman was a wise woman, she was also a humble woman, for humility is part and parcel of wisdom. And since she was humble, she did not include her own profession among those she considered to be of greatest service to mankind. "I'm just a housewife and mother, that's all," she would say.

But her sons have come to know better!

They recall too well the many cuts and bruises that were soothed and healed under her direct care—the rusty nails pulled from tender feet—fingertips literally squeezed back on the hand after dangling by a thread. And there was the time she stood watch for three days and nights to battle a ravishing fever that had come to take its toll in death. Indeed, she belonged to the honored medical profession.

They shall never forget those wonderful evenings when a low, soft voice read on and on from the great classics of adventure and romance and history—pausing from time to time to describe a word, or draw an example from her own family environment. Without knowing it, she was the greatest of teachers.

Then there are the indelible impressions of her religious faith—the true values of life so clearly delineated—the on-going determination to be found in hope —the power and influence of prayer. It was evident in her singing of the simplest hymn, in the pronouncement of her creed, in her communion with God. It was a part of her daily words and deeds. It was in her eyes, her face, her walk, the work of her hands. No clergyman ever did more in line of duty.

Just a housewife and mother? No. Rather, the best of all three professions which she considered most worthy in the life of man! Doctor, teacher, clergyman— wrapped together in one, the most honored and worthy of all professions.

A Queen at Heart

CONNIE WAS THE MOST POPULAR GIRL in her school. She was pretty, talented, and had the happy trait of being a friend to everyone.

She was a good student, had been a class officer, and excelled in school activities. There wasn't any question that she would be elected May Queen. She was sure to be the first choice of boys and girls alike.

But Connie had other ideas.

She knew that within her class was another girl who wanted more than anything else to be May Queen. Connie did not know exactly how she knew this to be true but something told her it would mean a great deal to her classmate to be chosen for the honor.

The other girl had not been particularly popular. She had a few close friends, but she hadn't participated to any great extent in school affairs, so, consequently, was not well known throughout the student body. It would be difficult to elect her, unless someone did something about it.

Connie went to work. Quietly, she campaigned among her friends in each class. She pledged them to pass the word along for her candidate. She followed through on all the details to be sure nothing slipped up in the nomination and voting.

On election day, the other girl—Connie's candidate—won by a large margin. She was the new May Queen. And she had not known at any time who was responsible for her election.

But Connie did not stop there. She had elected a queen, so now she wanted her queen to be the happiest, most radiant queen the school had ever seen.

One of the other girl's problems was a proper dress to wear for the school dance the night before May Day. She would need to look her prettiest at the dance when she would be formally introduced to her classmates for the first time as their new queen.

Connie had such a dress. It was a new dress she had been saving for a special occasion. It was a perfect dress for the other girl. Carefully, she pressed it, folded and boxed it, and took it to the home of the girl.

"Every time I look at this dress, I think of you," she said. "Won't you wear it to the dance?"

The girl was overjoyed, but her happiness could not match the feeling deep down inside Connie when she saw her classmate—the girl who wanted so much to be May Queen—stand and bow to her "subjects" the night she was introduced at the dance. She was lovely, beautiful, the most radiant queen the school had ever seen.

There were two queens in the school that year. One was crowned 'mid a fanfare of trumpets. The other was crowned 'mid the quickening beats of her heart.

The Top Rung

NEVER HAVE THE GRADUATES coming out of our high schools and colleges had it so good! Business and industry are competing for their services. There is a shortage of engineers, accountants, teachers, nurses, skilled technicians and secretaries.

Later will come the first day on the job, and with it, some interesting discoveries. The new employe will find the competition among employers for his services has become a competition between himself and his fellow workers. Who will win out? Who will get ahead? Who will succeed?

Those with an extra measure of skill—yes. Those with unusual talent and ability—yes. But an important thing the new employe will discover as he goes along is that skill and ability alone are not enough to reach the top. True worth in a worker calls for qualities above and beyond dexterity of hand and cleverness of mind.

There are no short cuts in job progress. There is no easy way to a lasting promotion or advancement. There is no such thing as success based on material gain alone.

Many temptations face the new employe in his efforts to get ahead. Honesty may not always seem the best course to follow. Taking an unfair advantage of a fellow worker sometimes appears to be the wise thing to do. Cutting corners in the quality of work performed is a constant test of loyalty.

But we cannot live by two sets of standards, one geared to our work and the other to the balance of our life and living. We cannot separate what we do on the job from all else that we are and do. Honesty, fairness, loyalty, and the courage to do right are not qualities that can be turned on and off as we see fit to use them. Either they prevail in every act and deed, or they do not prevail at all.

The young men and women coming out of school every spring face a challenging opportunity. But it would be well for them to remember three important things as they begin their job careers—

Work is one more of the many ways we are called upon to worship God. We praise Him when we do our work well as surely as when we kneel in prayer or sit in the church pew.

Work is part of God's plan for man. He is the giver of our talents. We glorify Him when we develop and use such talents properly.

A relationship with God is the only phase of an occupational career where we can start at the top. And cultivating that relationship is the only sure way to rise above the lower rungs of the ladder.

A Pilot Light

OCCASIONALLY, we hear someone say, "What good does it do for one man to try to change things? One man can't do much when it comes to this business of applying the principles of a religious faith to the situations he encounters in everyday life!"

For an answer, let's look first at what happens in a large convention group or public gathering when the single match test is used to prove the importance of the individual. No doubt you have been a part of this test at one time or another.

All lights are turned down until the gathering place is in total darkness. Then each person present is asked to take a match from his pocket and hold it until the signal is given to strike it. On the appointed signal, each individual strikes his match, and the whole place lights up as bright as it has ever been.

It is true, one match alone does not make much dent in the darkness. But, by the same token, each match that isn't struck diminishes the amount of light produced. Each individual, the light he can throw, large or small, is important to the overall result.

We do not hesitate to apply this principle to other phases of our lives every day. We believe in the importance of the individual doing his bit, accepting his share of responsibility, in his job, in his home and family life, on the playing field, and in civic and community endeavors.

We do not say, "What good will it do for me to do a good job? There are others where I work who don't seem to care!" We do not give up trying to make our children into fine citizens, simply because other families neglect this obligation. A great baseball pitcher on an otherwise ordinary team continues to pitch his heart out to win. Important elections have been won because one more voter in each precinct decided it was worth while to go to the polls and cast a vote.

The individual and his personal influence are essential in every facet of life and living. He need not feel that it is up to him to set the entire world on fire. He need only light up the little area around him. Then, with the example he has set, others follow, and a whole city, state, or nation takes on a new brilliance.

A pilot light is a very small flame, but without it we are helpless in igniting the larger fire that generates power and warmth and influence as we seek a sense of security and well being.

Each of us can be a pilot light, capable of setting off a combustion that can change the life of a friend, neighbor, or fellow worker, and, thereby, add to the sum total of good in the world.

Broken Figurine—A Parable

PAUL HAD BEEN GONE almost an hour, but Betty still sat at the breakfast table staring into her half-filled coffee cup.

She had dreaded this moment. She had been afraid of it. They had been drifting farther and farther apart recently, and now the break had come.

She told herself she did not know why. But she did know why! Paul was selfish and self-centered! He insisted on everything revolving around his interests! Whatever they did together, it had to be done his way! And she had come to resent always giving in to him. And he knew it!

They had quarreled last night over nothing more than a television program. The quarrel had continued this morning at breakfast. Paul had said he was going to talk with a lawyer. Perhaps he would be home tonight—perhaps not!

She heard the back door open and close, and footsteps coming through the kitchen. She recognized the walk.

"Anybody home?" her mother called.

Betty waited.

"Well—what's wrong here?" her mother exclaimed, as she entered the dinette. "It's nearly ten o'clock and breakfast dishes still on the table! This isn't like you, Betty. Was Paul late this morning?"

"No—left at the same time," Betty answered.

Her mother turned to the credenza for a coffee cup. "Why, Betty—what happened—your finest china figurine—here on the floor—broken!"

"Paul knocked it off as he was leaving," Betty answered, guardedly. "It was an accident."

Her mother stood looking at the pieces of china scattered on the floor. She knew her daughter too well to think she would be upset over a broken figurine.

"It looks as though someone will have to do a piecing-together job around here," she said, finally.

She gathered up the broken figurine in a napkin, brought a tube of cement to the table, and methodically set about fitting the pieces in place.

"You know, my dear," she said, as she worked, "when something like this happens, you must take care of it right away, or the pieces might become lost, and you wouldn't be able to put them all together again.

"Almost always, you will find, you can repair this sort of thing so you would hardly know anything had happened. But you must get to it before it is too late, even if you feel you weren't to blame in the first place.

"And you should understand, Betty, very often it is someone other than the person who does the breaking who must do the mending. It is always worth the effort, if you really want to preserve the finer things you have."

Cradle of Liberty

As WE APPROACH the Fourth of July, let us do so with a deep sense of appreciation and reverence for the religious influence that dominated the thinking of the founding fathers of our country. For, without it, the pattern of government laid down 180 years ago would have been nothing more than an instrument of insurrection, and our nation would not have survived to stand today as "the one great hope of freedom" throughout the world.

History provides a wealth of evidence that the men who molded our national destiny were men whose faith in political liberty was anchored to a faith in religious liberty. They saw no difference in the two. Freedom was freedom, whether it sprung from legislative halls, economic pursuits, or the church pew. And the significant point is that religious principles were the cause, not the result, of the governmental mechanism that crowned their efforts.

Of the 55 signers of the Declaration of Independence, one was a clergyman who has been described as "an animated son of liberty." Another had been an active clergyman, and still another was an army chaplain. Two were noted for their philanthropy to church causes.

Outstanding church laymen of the day are known to have brought their influence to bear on George Washington, John Adams, and other colonial leaders. Washington's personal secretary and the secretary of the Continental Congress were such men.

Church groups of the day provided an invaluable factor in welding the young colonies together in the common cause. Whereas each colony was a separate political unit with no central authority or purpose, church congregations had already established interlocking organizations that swept across territorial lines and unified their memberships. In the beginning, these groups were the only medium of interest and understanding among the people as a whole.

The purpose of the Pilgrims finally paid off in 1776. Their hardships and struggles, endured in the faith that freedom to worship was a God-given right, paved the way for a total freedom that was to dignify the individual in every facet of life in the new country.

Throughout it all, in Philadelphia many years ago, the godly men among those who framed our future held to the hope that the problems of the day could be resolved within the bounds of peaceful procedure. But once the violence of war, supported by a just and righteous cause, was inevitable, they lent their total strength to the effort.

In the words of one of them— "There is no soldier so undaunted as a pious man."

Antidote for Worry

WORRY IS SO MUCH A PART of life these days, there are actually people who feel restless and lost if they find themselves suddenly without something to fret about. "I can't understand what's wrong," they say, "I haven't a thing on my mind."

We cannot hope to escape problems entirely, but surely we are not supposed to subject ourselves to constant mental and nervous strain by looking for troublesome questions to solve. Most of them aren't important, anyway, and the more we learn to eliminate them from our lives, the better able we will be to cope with the truly serious ones.

A good practice for the chronic worrier is to make a list of all the things he thinks he should worry about. Set them down one by one. Make a long list. Include every possibility, great and small. Then go through the list and analyze each one. Is it worthy of worry? Does it measure up in importance? How does it compare with the others on the list?

Interestingly enough, when the complete list has been covered, and the unimportant items have been crossed off, there will be only two or three that require any real thought and attention.

Then comes the second step. The worrisome items that are left are problems that either can be solved or cannot be solved. The ones that can be solved require no worry. They need only a proper plan of action to do away with them. The ones that cannot be solved will not be helped by worry.

It is always helpful, when considering the problems in our lives, to think also of the blessings or good things that surround us. Make such a list. Include the values and benefits of a home, children, friends, church associations, a job, the advantages of life and living as compared with others we know or have known, both today and in years gone by.

Here we find nothing we want to eliminate. The list remains long and grows longer as time and thought add to it. In contrast to a list of worries, it is impressive and convincing.

Our tendency is to overemphasize trouble and de-emphasize the recurring benefits that come to us day after day. An old and very wise writer put it this way recently, "Grief counts the seconds while happiness forgets the hours."

Grief is penetrating and worry is great in time of real and intense trouble. Happiness slips into our lives and glides along so smoothly and consistently, we are inclined to take it for granted.

When adversity, genuine and severe, finally comes, as it is sure to come sometime in life, there is one great source of hope always open and available to us. But we must know our troubles for what they are, real or imaginary. We cannot expect God to solve riddles.

Where You Find It

THERE IS AN OLD SAYING to the effect that you usually find what you are looking for. If it is trouble you seek, you can find it. If it is evidence of good in the world, abundant testimony is waiting. It's a case of what you want, what interests you. You are sure to find it if you start looking.

In no way does this prove out quite so conclusively as in the search for signs of religion at work in the world. We hear a great deal about the growth in church affairs and the application of religious principles to everyday life. But, beyond increased church member-ship and attendance, and a mushrooming expansion of church facilities, we do not always see evidence of a profound faith and conviction on the part of the indi-vidual. That is, we do not see this evidence until we start looking for it.

A businessman was asked not long ago to give a television talk on the importance of religion in his life. He arrived at the studios a few minutes before he was scheduled to go on the air. The staff on duty at the time showed no particular interest in him or his subject. To them it was another routine program, or so it seemed to the businessman.

When he had completed his broadcast, much to his surprise, the announcer, director, producer, and engineer gathered around and, together, they discussed his talk and exchanged views on their religious beliefs. Each was a man of firm faith in God.

A small group of men in one of America's great cities decided to experiment with religious services in industrial plants and office buildings. It was a bold decision. There was no assurance their efforts would be well received. In fact, the evidence was to the contrary.

The result to date has been next to phenomenal. Prayer sessions are a regular part of the business day throughout the city, and wives left at home have caught the spirit and turned the mid-morning "coffee break" into periods of devotional worship.

Recently, a committee of young executives in a large company met for the express purpose of considering the question— "Should we set up a religious program for the employes of this company while they are on the job?" There was some fear that even the membership of this small committee would say "No."

Following the discussion the group adopted a specific set of recommendations for establishing such a program in their plant. As one man put it—"good human relations among men are impossible unless founded on religious principles. A religious faith is the base from which you start."

These are evidences of an expanding interest in religion sifting down to the individual in his routine life. There are many more about us, waiting to be discovered, if we will but look for them.

A Major Decision

SOME FOUR YEARS AGO, a young man finished law school and enthusiastically set about earning a living as a practicing attorney. He was typical of young men on the business scene today. He had served in World War II, returned to school after the war, married and become a father. He was talented, ambitious, and had a winning personality that promised more than average success.

But he soon learned that building a law practice is a slow and discouraging process. Clients did not seek him out as readily as his financial requirements demanded.

Day after day he sat in his small office waiting for that first important case that would launch him on his career.

Finally, it was necessary for him to earn more money to keep going. He obtained a part-time job, one that permitted him to keep his office hours as a lawyer. But his income still was not sufficient, so his wife started teaching school.

Together, they managed to pay their bills. But life became a constant grind. The consuming hours of his part-time job, the problem of care for the child while the mother taught, plus endless waiting in the little law office, made up a tedious struggle for existence. The young man lost his confidence and courage.

About the time he decided to close his office and turn to an entirely different occupation, he received a call from a company which was looking for a young lawyer to handle its accident claims. It was a good-paying job with an excellent opportunity to advance to chief legal counsel. He made an appointment to discuss the position.

The hopes of his family soared. Here, at last, was the means of living a normal, satisfying life, the chance to be a full-time husband and father, with a full-time mother in the home.

The day of the appointment arrived. He sat with officers of the company and listened to them discuss the duties he would perform. They cited examples of claims that had been settled for half or a third of the amount of coverage, how the company had maneuvered to escape liability altogether in some cases.

The young man thought surely he misunderstood. "But, gentlemen," he said, finally, "what about these people who are injured for life—the families of those who are killed?"

"Your job," one of the officers answered, "is to settle claims at the lowest possible cost to the company, regardless of circumstances."

The young man rose to his feet. A calm strength came over him and brought with it a confidence and courage he had not known in months.

"I do not believe I would be interested in the job," he said.

That was almost a year ago. The young man is now busily devoting his full time to what promises to become a brilliant law career.

Effective Witnessing

We usually think of a witness as someone who appears in court and testifies in a law suit. Yet the term— witness—has a much broader meaning when applied to our over-all lives, the faith we profess in a Supreme Being and the laws for mankind as found in the Bible.

The witness in a court case swears to tell the truth. He calls upon the help of God to assist him in honestly and forthrightly relating what he knows about the case from personal knowledge and experience. He does not rely on hearsay or rumor. A good witness is a willing witness, one who is anxious to assist the court in carrying out an orderly process of law. His primary aim should be the establishment of justice.

In another sense—a very real sense—each of us is a witness to what we know and believe, what our personal experiences have been, in the cultivation and application of a religious faith. Every word and deed bears witness to what we are, the principles that guide us, the beliefs we adhere to in everyday living. Each incident in our lives is a "case on trial" in which right and wrong are being tested. It is our duty, as citizens of faith, to come forward on the side of right, and, thereby, add to the sum total of justice in the world.

Here, again, as in a court proceeding, we are not to rely on hearsay and rumor. What the world wants and needs from men and women of religious faith is not what has happened to someone else, but their own personal experiences.

We often hear about the other fellow, what a fine man he is, what he is doing for his church, his success in bringing up his family in a religious atmosphere, what he is doing to advance the cause of good in the community. But what has happened in our own lives as a result of following "the rules of the game"? That's what really counts when we "take the witness stand."

Most of us, at some time in life, have taken an oath—have sworn, so to speak—to live up to our belief in God and do all within our power to broaden the effect of His influence. One of the basic responsibilities in such a commitment is to be a ready and willing witness to the value of living a life as we know it should be lived. If we fail to do this, we fail as a witness.

It is characteristic of human nature to pass on to others information and suggestions we know will be helpful to them. We do it every day in many ways. But we cannot hope to set an effective example for others to follow if we confine our witnessing to material and temporal things only, and leave the spiritual forces that have meant so much to us out of our testimony.

A good witness presents all the evidence at his command in the interest of bringing the case to a fair and just conclusion.

Not To Be Regretted

MOST OF US CAN POINT to specific times and occasions in the past when we might have done something differently and, as a result, be in a more satisfying and beneficial position today.

We could have been smarter about a job offer, or used better judgment in connection with an investment, or taken advantage of an opportunity that would have completely changed our lives. We might have gotten more education, or saved more money along the way, or done a better job of raising our children. In any event, we think we might have lived with more ease and less trouble.

We sometimes take such matters very much to heart. "The one big regret in my life—" we say. Or, "If only I had it to do over again!"

Actually, there is nothing to be gained in censuring ourselves over things that are past and gone. If we genuinely and sincerely regret a lost opportunity or a misdeed, we can still use that experience as a basis for going on to a fuller and more complete life in the future. And, if we make a fair and impersonal appraisal of things not to be regretted in our lives, we find we do not have so much to regret after all.

Certainly we do not regret having friends, their kindnesses to us, or the times we are considerate of them.

We do not regret the returns we receive as a result of the work we are called upon to perform.

We do not regret the days we feel well, full of exuberant health and a zest for living.

We do not regret friendly advice and criticism, either in or out of the home, from those we know honestly seek to help us.

We do not regret the fulfillment of our daily needs for survival, the necessities of life which are so often taken for granted.

We do not regret that the sun came up this morning, that the world is moving in an orderly fashion, that the winds and the rains come to serve their purpose, and as long as these phenomena continue, all will be well.

We do not regret that God is a benevolent God, that the teachings of the Bible are universal in their application, that there is such a thing as the power of prayer.

These are things not to be regretted in our lives. We can live with them. We cannot live with our regrets.

The Big Test

RECENT TESTIMONY BEFORE A U.S. Senate committee investigating Communist brainwashing tactics brought an almost unanimous response from witnesses that a deep religious faith is one of the best hopes for resisting this evil practice.

One American serviceman who had been a prisoner of the Chinese Reds declared he had stuck so stubbornly to his faith that his persecutors were baffled, and finally "kicked him out" of North Korea because they did not know how to cope with him.

This confirms the story of an American missionary who was released from a Chinese prison camp not long ago. For months he was subjected to unbelievable torture and abuse. He suffered inhuman dignities and privation. Yet he stood his ground, maintained his poise, and literally dared the Reds to put him to death. He openly scoffed at the idea they could do anything to hurt him, so strong was his faith in God's protection.

Unfortunately, all prisoners of war in such situations have not been so fortified. They are the ones who have "cracked up," gone over to the enemy, signed false confessions, and generally collaborated in the campaign of hate against their homeland and fellow countrymen.

It is not necessary to fall into the hands of a ruthless enemy and go through a barbarous brainwashing to be subjected to such a test. Under less extenuating circumstances, but certainly nonetheless important to maintenance of character, we face situations almost every day in which it is wise to rely on a power greater than our own, and call on a strength greater than man has ever commanded.

Such tests come in the ordinary course of doing our jobs, in fulfilling our responsibilities to our families, in meeting the competitive forces that pull at us in every phase and facet of living.

In most cases, these tests are not of major proportion, but they prove an ability "to take it," as surely as the most vicious brainwashing routine. The man who knows where he stands and feels secure in that knowledge will win out eventually over those who would pull him down to their level.

There are many qualities that show on the surface of a man strong in character. He is selfless in his interests and ambitions. He lacks suspicion. He is emotionally mature and unafraid. But the quality that undergirds all of these is the quiet preoccupation of a relationship with his Maker that renders all other consequences of life to a relatively less important position.

"There is nothing you can do that could possibly hurt me," the POW said to his captors. He was a free man even before they gave him his freedom.

But he did not wait until that moment to build the

faith he called upon. He had built it through the years, in bygone days, by meeting and conquering lesser tests. It was ready, then, when the big test came.

What Our Churches Need

WHEN OUR CLERGYMEN return to their pulpits from their summer vacations, once again they will plunge into a busy round-the-clock schedule—the fall roundup of members and organizations, the challenge of Christmas, the coming of the new year and its new program, the Lenten season and Holy Week, and, then, another summer.

It is truly a full-time job that faces them, for they are on call 24 hours a day to advise and counsel, comfort and correct, inspire and prod. Their days begin at eight or before, and they never know when they leave their homes in the morning at what hour they will return.

They are all things to all people in their congregations and the communities they serve. They deal with moral questions, social problems, civic endeavors, business decisions, sickness and health, and birth, marriage, and death. Through it all, they want nothing more than for mankind to accept and practice, wholeheartedly, the principles of the good life as laid down through the infinite wisdom of the living God, as attested day after day in the lives of those who recognize His power and influence.

But the clergyman needs help. He cannot possibly do his job alone. He must have the help of his membership.

"But what can I do to help?" a member asks.

The answer—you have talents and skills which you use in your daily life and occupation. There's a place for these talents and skills in the program of your church. You can put them to work to help your clergyman do his job. That is all you are expected to do in your church—what you do and do well outside your church.

If you are a banker or accountant or lawyer, there is work awaiting you in your church.

If you have the ability to teach, there is nothing your church needs more.

If you can write or sing or print or cook or sew or paint or sell, or build things, or make things grow, your church has a job for you.

If you have patience and understanding and a skillful approach to the problems of those who suffer from pain and trouble, your clergyman has a list of calls for you to make.

Oftentimes, we have the idea we want to be something else when we take off our work clothes and turn toward our church doors. This isn't what God wants or what our churches need. He wants only that we give back to Him a portion of the talent and skill He has endowed us with in the first place. This is what our churches need. This is what our clergymen want from us.

The Route to Reward

ELBERT HUBBARD, who is best remembered as the author of *A Message To Garcia,* compiled and published a scrapbook of wisdom and common-sense sayings which was popular reading early in the century.

One of Mr. Hubbard's bits of advice was— "If you work for a man, in heaven's name work for him! If he pays you wages that supply you your bread and butter, work for him—speak well of him, think well of him, stand by him, and stand by the institution he represents."

Many things have changed in the relationship of employe and employer in the past fifty years, but the principle expressed in the foregoing quote is as sound today as it has ever been. It is still the essential approach to getting along in a job. It is practical, everyday religion at work in the process of developing a mutual benefit and respect between a man and the place where he works.

It is no more right for a worker not to give his best effort to earn the wages he is paid than for an employer to pay him less than he is worth. If the employer fails in this responsibility, the employe is not relieved of his responsibility. If the employer is wrong, it doesn't make it right for the employe also to be wrong.

There is far too great a tendency these days to carp about the job that produces the paycheck, and to criticize the man or woman who bosses that job. There are too few signs on the horizon that a deep and lasting loyalty exists between company, management, and fellow workers. There is too little pride in doing a job well, and too little ambition to rise above the average.

We are not meant to live and work in the middle ground of mediocrity. We are meant to apply ourselves, to the best of our individual abilities, to the work at hand—to use and develop our knowledge and skills to the fullest. Anything less is a violation of the trust our Maker placed in us when He gave us hands and minds with which to work.

Nothing is more appropriate to this theme than the Biblical parable of the talents. One worker loafed on the job and did nothing at all with his opportunity. The other two made the most of what they had, even though their abilities and resources were not equal.

Which one was the complainer, the worrier, full of fear and frustration? Which was caught in the dull monotony of failure?

Which were happy, proud, confident, glorified, rewarded?

In Defeat or Victory

THE MICHIGAN STATE DRESSING ROOM was a bedlam of riotous confusion. A field goal in the final minutes of play had given the Spartans a 17-14 win over UCLA in the annual football classic, the Rose Bowl. It was a long-sought victory, a proud achievement, a time of triumph.

Head Coach Duffy Daughtery made his way through the milling crowd that swarmed the field, and joined his players in the dressing room. "You were wonderful!" he told them. "God bless you!" Then he quieted them down for a moment of prayer.

Why? Why this interruption? Wasn't this a time for whooping-it-up—back-pounding—shouting congratulations? Wasn't this something to celebrate?

Here is Daugherty's answer:

"We open and close each game with silent prayer. Each one of us prays in his own way, according to his faith.

"We don't pray for victory. Victory is something you have to earn by going out there and working for it.

"We pray for strength—strength of character—a willingness to sacrifice, to be unselfish, to let the other fellow carry the ball and star.

"We pray for a unity of purpose, teamplay and spirit, the desire to win fairly, to win with honor.

"We pray that no one will get hurt, that we will play a clean, hard game, and if we are the best team on the field, that we will win.

"This is important," he added, "win, lose, or draw! Certainly, it is important when you lose. There is nothing quite like it to unite a group of boys again in a single purpose, to eliminate any hard feelings that may have come out of the game.

"But it's even more important when you win. It brings the players back to earth, gives them a sense of pride as a team, points up the value of sharing honors with others, gives credit where credit is due. By the time the boys get through their prayer, they are humble in victory; there aren't any individual stars."

Duffy Daugherty says there isn't any such thing as a self-made man. We all depend on one another to get where we want to go. Whether on the football field or out in the business world when school days are over, we must work hard, co-operate with others, do what is best for the game.

He denies that college football builds character. "If a boy doesn't have good character when he comes to us," he says, "likely as not he won't get it on the football field. Character is built in the home and church, before he gets to college. A good football team is a bunch of good citizens to start with. You can't win with 'bad apples.'"

Duffy Daugherty, voted the outstanding coach of the year, did *not* interrupt the dressing room celebration of his players following their Rose Bowl victory. He added to it by passing on the final decision on their performance to the greatest Referee and Field Judge of all.

ist, Congregational and other denominations. Most local churches have
a men's club or chapter dedicated to
the purpose of applying the principles
of their faith to the daily job interests
and occupational pursuits of the membership. Mr. Carr's columns follow this
theme on a non-denominational basis.

Some of Mr. Carr's columns have
been reprinted in national magazines,
trade association journals, and other
newspapers. Others have been quoted
on radio and television programs and
from pulpits. Clergymen have found
them a timely source of material for
sermon topics.

The Author

Eugene Carr is a businessman with
a long and varied record of civic and
welfare organization accomplishments.
He is director of radio for the Brush-
Moore Newspapers and president of
the Ohio Broadcasting Company of
Canton. Mr. Carr is currently president
of the Board of Trustees of First Presbyterian Church, Canton, Ohio and is a
member of the executive committee of
the National Council of Presbyterian
Men. Writing is his avocation and his
first book, HOW TO MAKE THE
MOST OF YOUR JOB was published
last year. Mr. Carr is married and has
three children.